How To Attract Women

Christian Dane

Table of Contents

How To Seduce Women

Christian Dane

Copyright © 2012 Christian Dane

INTRODUCTION

Since the main books on seduction had been disseminated, the use of methods to activate females, and consequently their comprehension, continues to be the subject of countless objections and disagreements. one among the immensely frequent challenges alleges that the work of a method would indicate that everyone's female square measures a comparable. The reply to the current rather objection is simple: any sort of social exploration is started about the observation of reiterated behavioral buildings. Ultimately, the proof that there's such a situation as science doesn't recommend we've got a tendency to most comprise exactly the same feelings and emotion. the precise comes about with seduction. Notwithstanding sex, absolutely no 2 individuals square measure similar, nonetheless, most manifestly discussed behavioral qualities. Another quite standard criticism is the fact that seductiveness is inherent, and also it can't possibly be tutored. Those which illustrate this sort of argument seem to be ignorant of the evidence that throughout their existence males and also ladies amass and develop methods in which of seducing. many mates without recognizing, a little analysis to achieve it, and many produce their strategies. I speculate nobody will flatly determine if a method is terrible or good, nonetheless, possibly they will be gauged on the target of its effectiveness. Your methodology might also be supported by shopping for flowers, dancing, taking part in connect amount instrument, complimenting, being, or lying utterly honest.

THE BEST WAY TO FUNCTION AS THE MAN

A hot lady is going to meet several regular people daily. She might pick any of them on the out chance that she required. Be that as it might be, what she hungers to be a real Man. Moreover, here is to contort That Man is not a real Man for her by yourself, however for every other woman as well. He's characteristics to that all young women will react. It is weird inside them. He's currently the one

in the intense scenario. This way, at a lengthy final, she must accomplish the grimy work and allure him. Ladies, do not experience hours before the mirror simply to be sure they set their greatest person ahead, yet along with guaranteeing that when a genuine Man comes, he views them or without his cash, and that's precisely how excellent seduction looks. The male chooses first, he communicates his enthusiasm for the person

7

through his concerns. On the out chance that he's powerful enough, the person is going to like him. At any rate, she'll as well recognize his Choices, therefore she is going to attempt to encourage the Man and workable him to stay with her. So I do not have my significance by "incredible"? Looks, cash, impact, or acclaim? Nothing, unless you find some other options. They're just shallow characteristics that can fool a person into feeling that you're amazing. Genuine pressure originates from within. A genuine man is going to cause her to feel like a lady just by the essence of his. Regardless of whether he's stripped or without his cash, garments, and vehicles, his capability emanates from within.

Back to development, the most significant point to show your lady is that she can have a feeling of security with you. A man should be adequate to lead her. At any rate, in case you're within an eatery and she's the individual that must take the table in which you sit, at that time must organize the food while tuning straight into the say of yours, "You are very charming. I do not merit such a stunner," what'd she believes Is this male furnished for securing her? Does she have a sense of protection with him? No. And so the number one quality a person has is the capability to direct.

Listed here are the various other three as well:

1. A male knows how to lead, and he's positive in his role.

2. A man usually has self-respect, and options are never needy.

3. A male knows how to treat her.

Let's look at No. one again: A male realizes a how-to guide, and he's sure about his job. Your expertise is hard, is it to be the chief of a motorboat? You're constantly compelled to settle for options and take on duties. A small indication of vulnerability is adequate for you to shed the confidence of your entire group and almost certainly the boat as well. How could forty people follow their chief on the out chance that he provided indications of vulnerability and faltering? If you are on the team, okay hazard your life to this kind of commander? Not likely. Would you get it done for a particular and undaunted one who's Continuously certain, no matter whether he commits mistakes again and now? Certainly It is practically the same as females. You will find two individuals within a boat: you and her. You're the captain. She expects you to guide her. At the very first hint of uncertainty, she is going to jump out of your boat and pick another one. You'll continuously have to be on your toes when making decisions. Nobody cares if it is a bad or good decision; it is you who'll take responsibility in the long run. young guys cannot capture responsibilities. To be a guy, you've got to learn very first. Every choice you make can have consequences. You can leave making it, but later or sooner, you are going to have to choose.

I have not talked enough about trust yet. Postponement isn't a Manly trait. A male knows what he desires and is not hesitant to take it. When you make choices, be sure of yourself. It is a part of directing and taking obligations. You pick the restaurant in which you would like to go on your date. You pick the table in which you'll sit. There is a distinction separating false and real confidence. A confident individual is cool and calm, such as a sniper waiting for his turn in the bushes. When such a character steps into an area, everybody is gazing at him. And not since he helps so stiffly that they're giggling at him! It might be a falsely confident style, someone who's possibly annoying or funny due to visibly overreacting to his insecurities. Common symptoms are: getting recognition if it is obnoxious, harassing personage both physically or literally to build a thing to spectators or even being stiffly formal, and also walking like a robot with a significant expression alternatively of a look. Nevertheless, in case you do not have real belief yet, how are you able to fake it and never appear to be feigning it? Is this not a paradox? Not exactly. With this encounter, you are ready to Loosen Up in your Character and look very every day from the outside.

HOW TO SEDUCE WOMEN

COMMON ERRORS MEN MAKE

I'm sure some of you have had a date with a lady that did not go how you anticipated. That's the case with everybody. Simply realize it is not a question of some invisible cloud to follow you around. How females answer to you will depend on your Manliness and character. You will find collective mistakes males often generate when going out with a female. A great deal in the massive photo is counted by diminutive details. There's a small bit of inconsistency inside your Manly frame and you drop her. This is the thing that I will be talking about in this part.

The best error you can make is treating a female like she's different by placing her on a pedestal or even looking down on her as well as treating her badly. Many guys, on seeing an attractive female, "OMG, are like, she's very warm and gorgeous. I do not usually merit such a lady ..." Why? Exactly why don't you deserve her? Is it because she's sexy? In case she is above you by any means? No. Is it safe to state she's more than you? No. She's a person, much the same as you as well as me. Ladies request you to be somewhat above them. They like it when they can admire a male without merely because you're taller. Have propensities or characteristics that she can appreciate in you, most amazing of which are your ability and personage to direct her within the proper way.

Cash

A real male will not require a great deal of cash to tempt a lady. She is going to have a sense of security with him, and there'll be no requirement for additional money related help. Do not invest your cash in ladies or even give useless endowments. It is okay to welcome her with the motion pictures or maybe pay on the primary date. At any rate, in case you are doing, foresee that she ought to spend the second. If she does not offer it, demand she contributes. Attempts to not compel her to settle the whole bill in virtually any case; a male is continually someone of respect.

On the off chance, you spend over the primary date and she does not provide paying, in any event, the part of her on the second, that's a sign that you might have found a gold digger chick. Evade those. Burn through cash on a lady when you have to and not when she requests it. On the out possibility that she beseeches you to get her some new something or garments, immovably reject. Be that as it might, over the off-chance that you're seeing someone, you may wish to check her out in hot underwear and get some as being a current. Do you see the distinctions between the 2 edges? The very last is your choice and never something she "requested."

A note for an abundance of folks:

It is okay to waste cash on a lady at your level. In the event you feast at the most popular, most severe diner consistently and also you can deal with the price of it, do not take her to a few substandard spots. Bring her into your existence. If you simply drive an unrestrained car, like Ferrari, do not go on the date of yours by transport. What's more, ultimately, does not pay her off. In the function that she gets to request and requests lots in the existence of yours, deny it. Additionally, for people that are not all that well off, if you simply cannot stand going to a trendy eatery yourself, do not manage on a tight budget simply to carry a lady there. Choose a modest but sentimental spot instead of where nourishment is acceptable. And on the other hand, go for no-cost dates like a sentimental walk in the leisure center. Never endeavor to coat your cash in a relevant situation. If you've got an unassuming car, don't rent an exorbitant car for anyone to take to a female making the rounds. She is going to find a couple of remedies concerning your money related situation in the long term. Keep in mind: Women will esteem you since you're someone but are not contemplating your money.

Sense of humor:

In several investigations of females about the best person, humor pops up as one of the most fundamental ascribes for a male to have. Never be excessively honest on your dates. Appreciate your moment together, laugh at 1 another 's jokes, and also, when the state calls for something wise, disclose to her something amusing. On the out chance that she is pulled directly into you, she is going to chuckle at your lamest secondary schooling jokes and think you're an amusing person. And so do not keep down, and do not save a straight face for the whole time. Self-incongruity is also an extraordinary recognition to have. Have the choice to chuckle at yourself, not specifically at others. Lastly, grin. You can grin excessively. A male is liked by ladies that grin at a good offer. It leads both you and your little woman to feel fantastic.

Companion zone:

The idea that you worry about virtually everything in your connections with women is hearing: "Allows be companions, alright?" You do not require them as companions. I am certain you've just learned that line and also have a few young lady "companions." You may have used it on young ladies that did not fulfill your guidelines. Overall, those announcements mean you messed one thing up. To set it obtusely, you have been a pussy instead of a guy. Generally, you both get along often, with a female or maybe she gets over you faster at some point or perhaps another. You do not require that, is that not so? So stop acting the way that you did to arrive. is followed by potential reasons.

Dressing, computing, working with yourself:

It's crucial to be put, flawless, and great for your best self forward when meeting women. They encounter hours before the mirror to look incredible; we can, at any speed, be sterile. Shave every day, rinse your hair, use antiperspirants, clean your dick. This is basic data. Cut your nails and clean some dirt from under the nails on your toes. Use foot-antiperspirants should your legs smell horrendous. Clean your shoes every again and now, and reliably iron the articles of yours of clothing. Care about the shade of your socks, and do not mix them. Apply great apparel and shirts each day.

Such little subtleties are appropriate for girls. When creating your first link, they are going to survey you reliant on this particular link. Regardless if you do not view yourself as beautiful, there are certain advances you can take to put your ideal self forward. You do not have to look as though you ventured from several style magazines, nonetheless, a male realizes how to dress and what you should look as fine. Simply by doing that, he leaves a good effect on people. On the off chance you appear as though you are a geek, you are creating your own life harder.

And so take my recommendation:

Go to some beautician:

I suggest visiting the very best salon in the city of yours. Attempt not to spare cash on what looks like yours. Ask the beautician what hair he/she believes would be the best for your character and face. Simply by getting a cool and wonderful hairdo, you can change your image a great deal. In the event, that hair that long turns out to be emphatically for your face, wear it that means (yet continue it clean!). On the out chance that shorter or perhaps completely uncovered is better, choose that appearance. If you're inclined toward not seeing very much cash, go to the very best hair salon once, demonstrate your brand new hairstyle to the fortified beautician, and have him/her trim it in that way a quick period of your time later on.

Glasses:

They, generally, do not appear extraordinary. Put them in and use contact as the central focus. There are not a lot of men and women that appear extraordinary in glasses. If you've got to use them, endeavor to locate a couple that fits the state of your face. Shades can make you appear cool within late spring. Easily find them astutely. You can consult an agent at the dealer to aid you in finding a good pair.

Shaving:

Shave your face, or trim your facial hair. If you've got an inordinate degree of hair on your body, trim it or perhaps depilate it, making yourself appear smoother. It does not have some type of result whether you keep the pubic hair of yours or even shave it off, anyhow in case you ensure that it stays, make sure it is very trimmed and appears sleek. If sleeveless shirts are worn by you, shave your armpits.

Dressing:

This is probably the most crucial angle concerning your looks. Go to the most important club in the city of yours and examine how folks dress, in case you figure it might damage the image of yours, see what designs wear. Go to the closest purchasing network with 1 of your female companions (or, in case you've gone by yourself, ask the dealer salesman), for a few snazzy additional pieces of clothes. See plan twenty-four magazines or men's magazines. Constantly dress carefully. Find a style that fits your character, which is stylish all the while.

Working out:

Take upwards a game. If you are fat, get fit. I endorse slimming down which protein is different from carbohydrates (not being mistaken for low carb eating less, which can be very unfortunate) but still converse with your dietitian before doing anything insane. I also advocate turning into a veggie-lover, since it is beneficial for your wellbeing and leads you to make sure you are in balance. Be that here as it may, before anything is done by you, generally request guidance from a professional, or maybe counsel the correct books. If you're slim, put on several muscles. It is a shrewd strategy to appear buffed into a piece. You don't ought to be an additional Schwarzenegger but take extraordinary thoughts out of your body. If you'd favor never working out, use up hand-to-hand fighting or even moving. Both give exceptional direction on probably the most excellent strategy to do what must be completed.

Masculine non-verbal communique and voice tone My title is James Bond. Try not to giggle, even if the way they are truly fictional, you might see a great deal in James Bond campaign photographs. He's a Good Man. How about a tad played by us? Envision that you 'purchased the James Bond within an up as well as the upcoming film. Exactly how may you put yourself in place for it? You may presumably examine the great bulk of the James Bond films efficiently accessible along with exercising on the front side associated with a reflection to make your portion match the very first person impeccably.

Presently I don't request you check out all the James Bond films. Nevertheless, I request that you view a couple, and instead of focusing on the excellent interesting scenes, interest at the essential character. Find out how he strolls, how he talks, the sculpting of his voice, and how he communicates with women. What he says is not often excessively significant, but just how he says it you might have a lot from which. He's continually certain, easygoing and quiet. He knows how-to guide, and he knows that females will regularly tail him. I endorse your shift to your preferred video store today and also rent a few James Bond movies within the event that you have not only completed them as such.

Read her frame language as well as hunt for clues, both good quality as well as negative:

Okay, straight upwards, you'll not know this out correct away bro. Trying to read women is not continually smooth and you can experience as much as you want an overseas translator. Which you sort of doing since it might sense as ladies are occasionally from a distinctive world. Nevertheless, I am going to assist you to get this one out. Did you realize, that despite it often seems as if it's us guys that ought to make the method to initiate seduction with women, that ninety % of the time it is miles sincerely her? She is going to use motions to show whether she's happy for you drawing near her. It's frequently through the eye, dealt with and body indicators dispatched out to the concentrated male. If you are perceptive enough to pick up on the signals, you might be extra than possibly having an effective method.

Today, do not pass getting overly thrilled with the aid of this because many men aren't great at choosing up on lady frame words. We've got a great deal more testosterone floating around our bodies that might inspire us to often mistake a pleasant grin for sexual interest. What a minefield! A great deal of body dialect is subconscious mind as well as he or maybe she is going to be easily giving secrets and strategies left to right and center in case you research to protect a watch out for all the signs. Body language is such a big putt that a whole book might be dedicated to it.

Here's a listing describing self-confidence and Manly body words. Make use of it to adjust yours:

Eye Contact: A female who might like you'll typically appear your way, trap your eyes for a couple of seconds, and appear at bay once more. Check first if your zipper is not down and you don't have spaghetti sauce splattered badly on your shirt as a factor she's certainly looking at. If you're all great, she can duplicate this short look up to a couple of times. In repeatedly considering you and away once again, she's suggested a hobby in your method. The majority of the time, you've got to analyze the other individual inside the eyes. Do not stare at her awkwardly; just go for a glance here and there and protect eye contact when you might. Never gaze at the earth when conversing with someone either. Looking away from the edge, however, is by absolutely no means down. Confidence has to be radiating from your glance.

Smiling: It is generally clever attention to smile. It disarms people. Scientifically, it is settled that smiling will not just give high-quality sentiments on the person grinning, however, on the smiler too. This is you. Therefore, don't be unwilling to do it. You should not usually have a prime laugh all around, but, when talking with females or even moving toward a young lady, attempt to grin an amazing deal. It establishes a decent connection and motivates her to slacken in place at the same time as conversing along with you. She will not be as afraid as she might be over the off chance you drew nearer with a genuine look all over. And so don't forget about what I state, and also shed the macho factor, Ok?

A confident individual is designed for the most part in a beautiful and comfortable state. He abstains from making fast movements. He doesn't play with his hands or shakes his lower limbs anxiously. Each move you make and every muscle you move should function as the aftereffect associated with a cognizant preference without being brought around by a method of uneasiness. Walk steadily, but casually. Don't walk like a robot, in case it is currently not an over the top amount of difficulty be without proper care in the globe. You're not in a hurry. You do not wish to run. You are not being pursued. Move at your own pace. What is more often, don't be unwilling to occupy a couple of areas as you move. You'd choose now not to stroll together with your fingers unfolding six feet apart but display that you can occupy the distance close to you.

A selfish character is going to take all the room he can; a certain character takes as much as he needs, but wouldn't method authorization for it. Continuously be Ok with yourself. In an event where you're feeling amazing in a selected place, it'll probably be huge to others too. What's more, remember, that's ideal for training. Try not to be dumb, plus do not believe that the more you overstate the above mentioned, the additional Manly you might appear.

Yet another problem I have to speak about is my tone of voice. Some guys would perhaps have trouble with their voices. It's to originate from the chest/abdomen region and no longer from your throat. You can work out when you build yourself: Repeat pronouncing compliments like, "You have a lovely smile.

Posture: If she wants you with the technique, her posture could be placed to expose off. By this, I recommend she might be straightening clothes, flicking or touching her hair, and probably gently licking her lips. If she's sitting down, extra than likely she'll be sitting straight subsidized with legs crossed demonstrating to be above something she thinks are her exceptional assets. Likewise, in case she's standing she may also emphasize her curves by tilting her hips slightly forward. Remember, with most women who have been distracted and haven't, what they believe is outright blatant flirting. Do not pass almost like her, in case she's leading this kind of frame language, wondering if she's easy and maybe handled as such. You genuinely do not need her to be the first to influence her individuals to be sleaze since you come across body language the wrong way!

Speaking to her: If you're making a great opinion after approaching her she might also search for a chance to buy an opportunity to contact you. She may also repeat the touch to consider just how snug you've been with it. Here are a few good facial gestures to look out for when talking to her to enhance your self-belief that your very first method and influence are going very well.

Raised eyebrows: When mixed with a smile or maybe a nod, it often implies she's intrigued and concurring with what you're announcing or doing.

Active eyelids: It has among the cherished stereotypical women teased still at the off danger that if she's hanging her eyelashes at you she's becoming a tease back.

Dilated Scholars: It just operates in a lively setting. Both male and female pupils dilate (get darker and bigger) if they are talking to someone they are fascinated in.

Flared nostrils: This is an involuntary response that happens in women in case they can be aroused and excited.

Lips: Chewing or even licking her lips attracts your attention closer to them, which is a sexual or arousing part of her frame.

Arms: Collapsing your fingers is a shut spot. It implies which you can be concealing things, you are no longer happy, you'd choose now not to speak, or maybe you do not care for what another individual is stating. A certain Man is constantly agreeable and does not wish to shroud anything. As a rule, he has his arms through his sides or even somewhat in his pockets.

Legs: Shutting your legs, crossing them, or perhaps maintaining your toes collectively might display insecurity. Stay with your feet more giantly separated. A 4.5-foot journey would be crazy. Stay in a comfy, everyday way The items to be leery of as cues she's not fascinated by or perhaps has modified her mind about you are mentioned below.

Crossed palms: If she's crossed her palms probabilities are she's become uninterested or bored. She's setting a screen among your every and also you might wish to surrender attempting to flirt as well as converse.

Touching her hair in fast jerky action: Touching her locks in gradual gentle twirling or twisting is an incredible indication. Nevertheless, if it is being accomplished in fast jerky actions then in this likely fashion she's uneasy, embarrassed, and bored. Particularly true if combined with searching on another path.

Looking away: When she's keen on you she is going to display this via looking immediately into your eyes. If she's asking for everything, however, then it is time to offer up and you have misplaced her.

Women can show you plenty about their hobby in you without uttering a word. So be looking for cues and discover the right way to develop your making this work to the gain transferring forward. Not the handiest do you wish to discover ways to learn her, nonetheless, you also need to work to make a personal wonderful impression of yourself. This will come from increasing knowledge to understand frame language and also creating your own to succeed in her over and over a screen that you're in the track of the material. Keep in mind that this is merely a basic guide and no longer all females have an identical frame language. Additionally, sexual gestures such as licking lips are attained subconsciously; sex enchantment will be the brain 's herbal reaction in case you're inquisitive about somebody of the complete opposite sex. It now does not automatically suggest she needs to have sex with you. Reading her body language is a fantastic tool for you, but recall she might be performing the same, so it's crucial that you also give off the best cues to initiate flirting and make a good impact.

Here are some quick tips:

Smile: What've you got to lose in a fast smile? Even in case, she doesn't seem to have an interest, you are going to have possibly brightened her day. Smiling constantly makes you feel more optimistic and confident.

Stance: To make yourself look amazing, which is

provocative to most ladies, stay with your feet set broad apart and towards her. You can likewise put your hands on your hips to produce a great photo. Practice this particular within the mirror since you do not require it to fall off looking dorky.

Touch: She wants to know if you're serious too. So if everything is going very well and you've initiated the conversation, make a point of flirting by gently touching her reduced back, top arm, or perhaps waist. If she leans in, she'll likely be at ease with this particular one. If not, refrain from touching her once again until further interest is indicated by her. Girls do not love wandering, creepy hands, and wrists so exercise this one with extreme caution.

For starters, put things with each other on the inside; afterward, everything will be okay on the outside in case you would like to have success with women, you've to get your own life under control initially. If perhaps you're a nerd and do not have hobbies apart from sitting in front of the computer and watching porn, obtain a living as crude as it seems.

A male is passionate. He has dreams and objectives for his life, and he's driven to get what he wants. A person cherishes tuning in to a male that speaks enthusiastically about the diversions of his, work and also whatever. She needs to talk about his fantasies and be a portion of his great world. With the function that you do not come with an actual presence outside of the club in which you've become her, how might she be a portion of a thing that does not exist? She cannot. Imagine standing up on the dance flooring. You generate eye exposure to a female, walk up to her confidently, and request a dance. Then you get her hand out without waiting for a reply, point her to the dance floor and begin dancing with her. In such cases, you are going to FEEL what it is love to be a guy. The hot look in her eyes, the way she glances at you, wanting you to direct that is when you recognize what being a person means. You learn how to lead and make choices. You learn how to push and pull her with care. You learn about the slight power play moving on between the female and the male on the parquet. Do you feel what I am chatting about?

After you have done what you can accomplish your goal, let go of your obsession. Go out sometimes, socialize, make close friends, and live a fast-paced life. Once you forget what you needed so much, you will have females flocking around you. Time and patience are needed to become successful with women. The busier you are, the less time you have to feel sorry for yourself due to not getting females or perhaps not obtaining the ones you need, and the more likely that you will achieve success.

HOW TO SEDUCE WOMEN

THE SEDUCTIVE PROCEDURE

Almost everyone knows that specific steps on our part may have a seductive impact and a pleasing effect on anyone we'd love to seduce. The dilemma is that we're typically way too self-absorbed: We assume what we want from others compared to what they would want from us. Our attempts at seduction typically don't survive long enough to make much of an impact. You won't attract anyone by exclusively banking on your interesting style, or even by regularly completing something notable or even alluring. Seduction is a process that happens over time the longer you are taking and also the more slowly you go, the intensive you are going to penetrate the head of the victim of yours. It's an art that utilizes patience, strategic reasoning, and focus. You have to remain in stride in front of your victim, tossing debris in their eyes, casting a spell, trying to keep them off balance.

The seductive procedure might be regarded as a sort of initiation ritual, in which you're uprooting individuals from their habits, giving them novel happenings, placing them through examinations, before initiating them into a brand new life. At all costs, stay away from the enticement to rush to the climax of your seduction, or perhaps to improvise. You're not being sexy but greedy. Everything in daily life is hurried as well as improvised, plus you have to offer something different. By seizing your time and also appreciating the seductive practice, you won't merely digest your victim 's hostility, though you'll also make them look like autumn.

Stage One

Separation, Stirring Interest and also Desire

Your targets reside in their universes, their brains busy with daily burdens and pressures. The objective of yours in this first stage is usually to gradually segregate them from which closed world and fill up their minds with thoughts of you. When you've concluded with whom to reduce (one: Choose the appropriate casualty), your first task is usually to buy your preys' sympathy, to combine the passion for you. For the people who might be intense or insusceptible increasingly, you need to try a progressively slow slippery technique, first doing the fellowship of theirs (two: Create a phony sentiment of security method in the roundabout way); for all the individuals that are depleted and also much less intense to reach a far more theatrical strategy is going to work, both interesting them, along with a weird existence (three: Send diverse signals) or even seeming to be someone who's craved as well as fought over by others (four: Seem to be an issue of desire).

After the victim is correctly captivated, you have to revamp their interest into something stronger - drive. Desire is generally preceded by thoughts of emptiness, of anything lacking inside that requires satisfaction. You have to intentionally instill such thoughts, make your victims informed about the adventure and romance which are missing in their lives (five: Create a requirement - stir discontent and anxiety). The drive has to be stoked by subtly cultivating ideas in the minds of theirs, hints at the attractive delights that await them (six: Master the art form type of insinuation). Mirroring your target' s qualities, indulging them inside their desires, plus moods will appeal and gratify them (seven: Enter the spirit) of theirs. Without knowing exactly how much more, more, and happening off, their thoughts now center around you. The occasion has appeared to be for something better. Lure them with irresistible satisfaction or maybe adventure (eight: Create bait) plus they are going to follow your lead.

1- Choose the best Victim

Everything banks on the goal of seduction. Study your victim solely, and select just those who'll prove susceptible to your allures. The correct prey is those for whom you can their mindset and find something incredible in you. They're continually isolated or perhaps at the very least fairly unhappy (possibly due to current bad circumstances), or even could be easily done so for the contented individual is nearly impossible to seduce. The ideal target has a few practical qualities that draw in you. The powerful feelings this particular quality encourages will assist in creating your seductive maneuvers that appear to be far more organic and powerful. The ideal destination authorizes for the best chase.

Keys to Seduction: Throughout the way of life we discover ourselves having to persuade folks to seduce them. Many will be fairly amenable to our impact, in the case of just modest methods, while others appear to be impenetrable to our charms It could be that we learn this a mystery beyond the control of ours, but that is a terrible approach to fighting life. Seducers, whether social or sexual, would rather take the odds. As frequently as you can they go toward individuals who betray a little vulnerability to them and stay away from the people that can't be moved. Keeping individuals that are unavailable to you by itself is a smart path; you can't seduce everyone. On the flip side, you should actively hunt out the prey which responds the proper way. This will likely help make your seduction more enjoyable and gratifying. Just how do you identify your victims? By how they react to you. You should not spend a remarkable deal of target on their thorough responses - an individual who's attempting to gratify or maybe charm you are most likely playing to the vanity of yours and desires a characteristic during you. Many shows you're producing an individual who's ready to identify the influence of yours.

2- Make a phony Sense of Security Approach Indirectly

The seduction must start at a perspective, indirectly, so the target merely gradually becomes conscious of you. Disturb the boundaries of your respective targets life way by way of a third party, and appear to nurture a moderately basic relationship, moving gradually from good friend to lover. Plan an occasional "chance" meeting, as in case you and also your goal was destined to become acquainted. nothing is much more appealing than a sensation of destiny. Calm the goal into feeling protected, then strike. women that are different cherish evasive, hate-over eagerness. Thus, play tough get, quit boredom evolving. And do not let your requisitions sound overly confident of possession. Imply sex Disguised as a relationship.

Key to seduction: What you are after may be the capability to stride people down the road you wish them to use. Though the game is hazardous; the second they think that they're acting under the influence of yours, they are going to become upset. We're creatures who can't stand feeling we're heeding another person's will.

3- Send out Mixed Signals

Once individuals are knowledgeable of your presence, plus potentially vaguely fascinated, you have to facilitate their curiosity before it finalizes on another person. What's striking and apparent may entice their attention in the beginning, but that interest is usually short-lived; in the very long run, obscurity is immensely much more powerful.

Instead, the vast majority of people are much too noticeable instead of hard to work out.

Impart different signs: both delicate and extreme, both otherworldly as well as hearty, both cunning and innocent. A blend of characteristics shows profundity, that captivates a lot while it confuses. An intelligent, invulnerable impact is going to make people have to know more often, bringing them into the circle of yours. Create power that is such by suggesting something contradictory within you.

Keys to Seduction: Absolutely nothing is able to move ahead in seduction unless you are able to attract and maintain your victim 's curiosity, the physical presence of yours being a haunting psychological presence.

4- Seems to be something of Desire

Few are drawn to anyone whom others resist or may neglect; folks huddle around those who have captivated interest. We would like what others want. To entice your victims better and cause them to become hungry to have you, you have to develop a sensation of the desirability of getting craved and also courted by several. It is going to end up becoming an express of vanity for them to function as the unique item of consideration of yours, to earn you from a crowd of wooers. Develop a spirit of recognition by encircling yourself with members of other sex friends, present admirers, and former lovers. Establish triangles that stimulate competition and increase your significance. Develop a condition which foregoes you: if numerous have surrendered to your charms, there should be a reason. But what goes on next? Our brains are barraged with pictures not only from the press but from the condition of everyday living. A lot of these images are very apparent. You become only one a lot more stage screaming for awareness; your attractiveness will pass if you spark the significantly more long-term kind of spell making folks think of individuals in your absence. That implies committing their imaginations, making them believe that there is much more suitable for you compared to what they observe. Once they magnify your image with their illusions, they are hooked.

Keys to Seduction: We are a community of wildlife and therefore are extremely affected by the tastes and wants of many other individuals. Imagine a big personal assembly. You observe a lonely female who no one talks to every time, and who is roaming around with no business. Could there be any self-fulfilling isolation about her? What if she's alone? Exactly why in that situation did she avoid it? Right now there ought to be a description. Until somebody takes pity on this particular female as well as begins upwards for a talk with her, she is going to look undesirable.

5- Create a requirement - Stir Discontent and Anxiety:

A flawlessly satisfied individual can't be seduced. Discord and anxiety must be infused within your targets' brains. Incorporate within them thoughts of displeasure, and then unhappiness with their conditions and with themselves: their living lacks mission, they've wandered from the criteria of their youth, they've become boring. The emotions of deficiency you generate will supply you with the flexibility to instill yourself, making them look at you like the reaction to their problems. Distress and strain are formalized antecedents to satisfaction. Acquire to cultivate the demand that you can fill. No business owner is able to fall in love in case he is still somewhat delighted with who he's or even who he's. For this particular purpose, falling in like occurs far more frequently among people that are young, because they are greatly doubtful, uncertain of the worth, plus in most cases embarrassed of themselves. The very same thing is true for individuals of various other ages whenever they lose anything of their life when their youth ends and when they begin to grow older.

Keys to Seduction: Everyone dons a mask inside society; we pretend to get much more certain of ourselves than we're. We don't expect other people to glance at that doubting person within us. In reality, our egos and personalities are far weaker than they seem to be; they deal with up thoughts of emptiness and commotion. you should never mistake an individual's opinion of reality. Individuals are continuously vulnerable to being seduced, because in use everyone must have a sensation of uprightness, can feel something misplacing good inside. Bring their doubts and anxieties on the exterior therefore they may be led and also enticed going by you.

6- Perfect the Art of Insinuation:

Making your goals appear to be disgruntled and within the basic needs of your concentration is important, but in case you are apparent, they will find you through and grow defensively. Insinuations would be the ultimate ways of manipulating folks.

Key to seduction: Consider conversely the hardiness of insinuation and recommendation. It uses a lot of patience and art, although the outcomes are considerably greater than worth it.

7-Enter their spirit:

Play by the suggestions of like, whatever they desire, alter yourself to their moods. Play by their guidelines, anything worth what they crave and adapt yourself to their attitudes. Fascinated via the mirror photo you present, they will open up, becoming vulnerable to the small impact of yours. When you've infiltrated their spirit, you can get them into yours when it's much too late to defeat. Renounce your targets in every impression and manner, issuing them nothing to act against or maybe prevent. Have you ever been nervous about trying out soaking upwards your mistress? Convince her, she's knocked you nearly all of a heap with her stunning looks. If she's purple she's sporting, praise purple; when she's in silk in good health, a situation when silk fits her very best of many, you can in addition applaud her execution in bed and her talent for lovemaking spells away what turned you on. Art's ideal when concealed.

Key to seduction: Just how strong it is reaching

them is, rendering them to discover things beyond our means. We often continue the feeling that just in case they appear to concentrate on us, it's nearly all meaningless the phase it exhausts us; they go back to their ideas. We wasted our daily life butting up against people like they were stone wall structure area areas. But instead of moaning about exactly how misunderstood and also dismissing you, why not use anything different: rather than seeing others as indifferent or hurtful, instead of trying to master the primary reason they act just how they do, check them out for eyes inside the seducer. The appropriate way to lure folks from their natural waywardness, as well as self-obsession, is applying their spirit.

8- Make Temptation

Entice your primary aim deep into seduction by building the correct urge: a glance within the joys to come. Try finding out there that downside of theirs that fantasy is by using but getting discovered, and a hint you're competent to point them toward it. The future seems to be great with possibility. Facilitate a curiosity much better when compared with the concerns along with anxieties that pick it, and are going to heed you.

Keys to Seduction: Most of the special time, people struggle to maintain protection together with a feeling of stability in their lives. If they'd been frequently uprooting themselves in the goal of any unfamiliar person, or maybe a dream that surpassed them by, they couldn't handle the daily grind. They pack the earth with temptation. It addresses up nonstop stress. As a seducer, you can never misjudge people's hunt for a fact. You understand that their fight to hold buying their morning is weakening, that they're irritated by laments and doubts. It's hard being righteous and good, frequently having to control probably the largest desires. What folks really want is to give in on the drive to provide. That's the single best way to eradicate the stress in their lives. There is a great deal more to resisting motivation than relinquishing it. When your process is creating an urge, that's better compared to the morning variety. Understand: everyone has a principal vulnerable stage, from which various other stems. Their weaknesses include greed, vanity, monotony, several profoundly repressed inspirations and food cravings for forbidden berries which are new. They signal it inside a bit of information that eludes their thorough control: their style of garments, an offhand comment. Provide them with temptation that is great, tailored to their weaknesses, and being able to produce the drive to possess the pleasure you place on their figure an impressive deal more prominently than the issues and anxieties that accompany it.

Stage Two

Guide Astray - Creating Pleasure in addition to Confusion

Your victims are extensively intrigued, and their drive for you is also flourishing. Promising your victims, and likewise leading them to be extremely emotionally charged, provides them with the sense that they're living many fantasies you've stirred into their imagination (fourteen: Confusing reality and desire). By providing them with just a component of the fantasy, you are more likely to have them heading again for an impressive deal more. Focusing your attention on them as the substantial bulk of the earth ends away and also consuming them on the trip will point them as in length astray (fifteen: Isolate the victim) you've. There's essentially no turning back.

9- Have them in Suspense

The second individuals feel they know what to predict from you, it reduces the spell of yours on them. A single technique to rule the lured along and keep the edge is developing suspense, a calculated surprise. They will not foresee what goes on next. You are unavoidably one stride ahead and in command. Make the goal a thrill with a surprise modification of guidance. People value mystery, together with the reality that it is essential to lure even more into your snare. Act so that leaves them wondering, carrying out something they don't foresee from you will provide them with an amazing feeling of suddenness.

10- Make use of the Demonic Strength of Words to Sow Frustration

It is tough making people listen; we assimilate them with their intentions and thoughts and in addition, have almost no time for you. These are the benefits of the hot language. Infuriate people's thoughts with loaded utterances, go with them, reassure them of their insecurities, enclose their internal fantasies, charming phrases, and pledges, moreover not just are they likely to tune in for you, although they will additionally lower their will to overcome you. Keep your terms vague, letting them pick up into it whatever they wish. Make utilization of composing to blend up fantasies, and besides, create an idealized illustration of yourself.

Keys to Seduction: I cannot seduce you without expertise in getting outside your skin and also inside a distinct person's, penetrating their psychology.

The key to sexy language is not the words you utter and perhaps your attractive overall tone of voice; it is a serious change in perspective and habit. Stop thinking about the first thing coming to your mind, you've got to control the drive to prattle vent your opinions. The fundamental element is discovering the content as anything not for talking genuine thoughts and feelings, however for confusing, delighting, and also intoxicating.

11-Pay Attention to Detail

Extraordinary words and phrases, as well as fantastic motions, are critical: for what main reason might you say you're making a good effort to fulfill? The specifics of seduction, the concealed clues, the spur of the second stuff you are doing are often even more fascinating and uncovering. You need to learn how to divert the victim of yours using a horde of entrancing little customs. Create spectacles to mesmerize their eyes; fascinated by whatever they see; they won't notice what you're up to. Learn to recommend the proper emotions and moods through details. useful gifts tailored specifically for them, fashion along with accessories modeled to gratify them, gestures that display the time and kindness you're paying for them. Many of the senses are interested in the specifics you organize.

12- Poeticize Your Presence:

Essential problems happen in case you are by yourself in your goals: most likely the smallest view of help that you are not there, and also it is in addition, all over. Overexposure plus friend will cause this response. Remain ingenious, please allow me to know so that when you are out, they will yearn to find out you again, and in addition, will link you with pleasant views. Colonize their minds by changing over a fascinating presence with exuberant moments and significant distance accompanied by estimated absences. Attribute yourself with poetic images and objects, so that in case they think about you, they find out about you through an idealized team. The more you predict in their minds, the more they will envelop you within sexual fantasies. He who does not comprehend just how you can besiege a female, therefore, she seems to forget all things he does not need her to discover out, he who does not comprehend just how to poetize himself right into a female it is from her that whatever proceeds as he wants and remains a bungler. To poet yourself right into a female is a talent.

13-Disarm Through Strategic Vulnerability and Weakness

Too much manipulation on your part could raise doubts. The most effective way to recoup your trails is to make other people feel stronger and dominant. If you appear to be weak, susceptible, intrigued by another person, and not able to manage yourself, you are going to make your actions appear much more reasonable, less calculated. Physical shortcomings, rips, bashfulness, and paleness can help create an impression. To additional gain loyalty, exchange excellence for virtue: build the "sincerity" of yours by confessing several sins on the part of yours it does not need to be actual. Sincerity is much more substantial than goodness. Play the target, then change your target 's sympathy into like.

Keys to Seduction: We nearly all have flaws, vulnerabilities, frailness's inside our mental makeup. Perhaps we are shy or over-sensitive or even require attention regardless of exactly what the deficiency is, it is a thing we cannot control. We may try to compensate for it or even possibly to conceal it, but this is often a mistake: people feeling something inauthentic or perhaps artificial. Remember: what is typical of your character is inherently gorgeous. All those who exhibit zero deficiencies produce jealousy, dread, then anger. We want to thwart them to bring them down. Do not fight against your vulnerabilities, or maybe attempt to manage them, but put them into play. Discover how to alter them to strengthen them.

14- Confuse Reality and Desire

To compensate for all the problems in the lives of theirs, people spend a good deal of the time daydreaming, imagining a long-term chock-full adventure, results, and even romance. When you can produce the suggestion that through you they can live out their dreams, you're about to have them with the mercy you have. It is invaluable to start with reduced speed, adhering to their trust, and unhurriedly creating the ideal which conforms to their desires. Aim at secret desires which have been deterred or restrained, stirring upwards unrestrained feelings, clouding their powers of reason. Lead them enticed to the hassle of confusion exactly where they can't see the gap between illusion and reality.

15- Isolate the Victim:

The remote person is poor. By slowly isolating your victims, you cause them to become a lot more susceptible to the effects of yours. Their security might be mental: by animating their field of fantasy through agreeable points to consider as spent on them, you swarm out most of their brains. The isolation may also be physical: you snatch them away from their typical lifestyle, companions, family, and home. Let them have the feeling of being marginalized, they are providing one world behind them and immigrating to yet another. When divided like this, they have got no outside help, and in chaos, they are correctly driven adrift.

CONFERENCE GIRLS

Figure out your goals and what you will dedicate - most of it will depend on you The main activity of yours is figuring out what kinds of women you want Even the absolute best seducers to possess a certain team of women they are better with for instance, in case you are inside your 40s and looking for a female disco. To comprehend what you're attempting to find and build your techniques accordingly. You will find females that are younger and older women. They are very knowledgeable and much less well-informed. You're about to look for several of them in clubs and others at exhibitions, the theatre or perhaps your social circle.

Generally, more mature women are much easier to locate and also seduce. They're possibly individuals with an incredible sex drive and also an enormous degree of stress and wedded women who are tired of their spouses and their lives as housewives. As women acquire far more maturity, they start having fewer and fewer options. As you grow older, you're more likely to have progressively more. And therefore be patient. Youthful women will have an impressive deal more choices. They're likely to be prepared to choose from an insane assortment of men, especially in case they look fantastic. And therefore to summarize, the basic measures are one. Think regarding what you're like and also figure out what female type you enjoy and what attributes she has to have. Make sure you thank women for their actions at once and also be realistic. If you are a virgin, do not be considered a professional the following week or in bed, possibly the hottest Playboy version. You will need to put an impressive deal of time and energy into achieving your goals. Stay rational, and never ever aim at something you discover you can't have within the long term. It's recommended to get short-term goals and small successes rather than to own an enormous disappointment.

2. Consider where your type of woman might be encountered in your city.

3. Frequently at these events or places. Just in case you don't see what you're attempting to discover, look for step one or maybe 2.

4. Talk around the women you meet up with.

Never ever forget that women have to be a part of

your life, not your reason for existing. The outlook to avoid this is: "It feels safe and bright at home. I won't head out today, perhaps next time" Which moves on for months or years, while you continually fall directly into a depression. Ladies won't dart to your house; you're likely to need to head out and buy them. Thus leave the protection of your home and socialize. It's the initial step to excellent results with females: understanding how to be an interpersonal person. Even in case you've just moved to a neighborhood, escape the house, and also do something. Everybody has an interest or a hobby to show other people. I don't care what it really takes to get you outside, but make certain you accomplish it. Sign on to take dance classes or perhaps another language course; attend a sports club it doesn't matter. Go out at the second, 2 times or perhaps possibly three times a week, visit locations that are different, meet people that are new, and look fantastic in your skin. Finally, do not overlook the point that good results will not be available in one hour or perhaps two; you will need to attempt at it. Thus have this in the brain when developing your goals, and do not be disheartened in case success does not occur later on. With perseverance and time, you'll at last supersede. Conquering your fear of talking to strangers Anyone who is not used to advancing strangers has a fear of serotonin. That is typical. Several individuals are going to find it easy; many will think it is very hard to beat. It is as if you are an actor executing on stage for the very first time in the presence associated with an enormous market. You are going to feel your cardiovascular siphoning, butterflies in your stomach, and a feeling of foreboding deep in your soul. Even the readiest on-screen characters will be tense before heading before the market. Nonetheless, the thing that matters is they discover how to manage it. So 's what you must do also. Find out how you can control your dread and also the nervousness of going toward women you do not have a hint of. Ladies outsider's male, just how scary does that sound? You won't ever do that, set right? You'll, old buddy, you'll!

Female Emotion

"That female is a bitch, almost all she does is moan as well as complain. "The above quote is one thing I pick up from a fellow man of mine on a nightly and daily basis, both directed towards a girlfriend, a female they're "trying" to fuck, or maybe a female they haven't yet spoken to. Occasionally, it's probably the harshest realities that perform for the best lessons in life. If you're among these males, and you create a second thought to just how a female is a supposed "bitch", or maybe a "complainer" etc. subsequently this particular report is almost certainly for you. First, acknowledge, there's simply no such problem as a bitchy female, instead, merely a male that can't offer her what she needs and craves from you...presence!

Understand Your Position

state When you consider yourself as a male, what job do you designate yourself inside the relationship? In many cases, the 2 parties involved are on that autopilot that every other 's mental way and state of interaction isn't managed or perhaps made aware of. This particular has to change. Very well, 2 things have to change.

One: Become conscious of your specific response patterns strong towards her, and prevent the response through presence, or just breathe focus.

Two: Become conscious of her mental expressive patterns and the constant desire of her that you can provide her the presence of yours, through her dynamic outbursts.

You should start to be aware of your role and then follow through within which is powerful. I'd love you to start to see yourself because of the rock inside the relationship, or when around females on the whole. As masculine, this is your role. See yourself as a haven for your gorgeous female to hibernate too. You don't have to pay attention to a female for probably the most part since whatever they claim could be very irrelevant. I'd recommend not hearing a female in probably most cases. Ladies do not tune in to one another. They do something a lot more profound: They are feeling one another.

Feel your woman.

The words that females speak are most certainly irrelevant, which moves within the procedure of seduction, together with long-run relationships. She does not often have a specific comprehension of what she's thinking logically. Rather, she's selecting the most effective terms she can get in that specific time, to be able to mirror her psychologically plentiful thoughts that change within her just like the blowing wind. This could lead to her thinking certain hurtful things inside a short while of passion, that'll just really impact the ignorant male. You can't quite possibly ask a female just how she plans on being these days, and maybe even within that second. Winds respond "I do not understand, nonetheless, I fucking practice like"...and like a female, even asking the blowing wind such an amazingly uneducated issue will likely cause an argument! Asking a female "how are you currently feeling", angers her a lot, since you're essentially saying the lack of your awareness to her emotions. She needs you to find her. To believe her. Without needing to ask.

WHAT DETERMINES FEMALE'S ATTRACTION

Today males still provide great value to physical attractiveness, although we do not immediately associate sex with reproduction any longer. Women, on the other hand, paid far more focus on the personality, condition, and hierarchy of their potential mates, taking into account their need for defense and also the risks of survival a male represented. The presence (or perhaps absence) of these characteristics is perceived by females through the observation whether calculated or otherwise of male behavior. It's generally thought that it's material possessions that females consider sexy, when really in many instances what's equipped with sex appeal isn't his possessions, although characteristics which enabled him to get them. If a male creates an economic kingdom, it will not stay in his business where his charm lies, but in his personality and with the characteristics which enabled him to construct it, elements that can be found in his behavior. This is not to suggest that the female that decides this particular male will not like his empire and his power. Let us now picture the male's son, who inherits most of his patrimony, but who lacks his father 's capability to always keep the businesses running, are inclined to Mental Need in common, females are drawn to males that invest to the same or even to a lesser amount than they do. This's great since somehow it means the less we attempt, the more productive we'll be. As the phrase worries, "do a lot less, not more"... What's meant by "investment" will be the extent to which individuals sacrifice or even alter their feelings by getting others to prefer them. A classic blunder within the system of seduction is implementing excessively grand methods to impress a female, like obtaining her flowers or maybe a box of chocolate, purchasing dinner inside a fancy restaurant, and picking her up from her house for a day. If one has needy conduct, various other individuals are likely to recognize it. Not merely females. It's a commonly acknowledged fact that displaying a needy attitude can have counterproductive impacts in an employment interview, negotiations, or perhaps some other interpersonal interaction. Being capable of accomplishing something to impress a female believing in fear what you should tell her, attempting to arrange a great day, purchasing the flowers of her, purchasing the dinner of her, etc.is a signal of neediness. Because of this, the more you persuade yourself you do not have to do anything unusual to succeed in her over, the happier you are going to position yourself as a male of value that is high with no requirement for approval. This isn't to suggest that an individual cannot create a female a current, and perhaps buy the flowers of her, but this ought to be accomplished in case it's created from an individual, unselfish desire, not in hope of winning her approval. This provides a clear reason why males that give their all to females that haven't shown some interest often go wrong in their attempts at seducing them, although these females considered it to be a "nice gesture". In keeping with this, males that stay away from displaying too much interest and trying overly difficult, typically have a significantly greater success rate.

The more we attempt to maintain someone close, the trickier it is going to be convincing them to remain. Males are inclined to feel drawn to females whose amount of mental need will be lower or the same as theirs, also. When a female manifest much more of a concern in us, we are likely to find her much less appealing. Paradoxically, it usually occurs that not purchasing a female can make her wish to purchase us. Exactly why is that? Since individuals subconsciously put a better value on whatever is scarce. Being overly available could put her senses off. Contrarily, looking unavailable could make her feel drawn to you. That's precisely why, but there are lots of situations where the best shot of yours at attracting or perhaps making up with a person is doing nothing. Look the opposite way. Go on. Nearly all males that attempt to persuade females by taking them on pricey dates and purchasing them beverages are placing into practice a skillful kind of manipulation. This means they're dishonest about their intentions and they require female's approval and attention. What they're unintentionally thinking is that females are above them, and also they attempt to compensate for this with cash. True integrity is wanting nothing in return. Genuine integrity is among the characteristics of emotionally self-sufficient folks. This does not mean that purchasing someone a beverage is showing neediness. You will find individuals both women and men that make themselves appear psychologically self-sufficient, show minimal interest for other people, and are unreactive, and nevertheless end up involved in co-dependent or toxic relationships.

HOW TO SEDUCE WOMEN

THE 3 PRINCIPLES THAT INFLUENCE THE SUCCESS OF OURS WITH WOMEN

In this particular sector, we are going to analyze in detail the principal variables influencing our success with females. The very first concept involves lifestyle. As we've previously noticed, individuals are likely to connect with other people with similar lifestyles. The greater we cultivate our lifestyle; the more risks we are going to have to connect with females we love. The next basic concept is courage, that's saying, the number of females we dare approach, just how many females we opened up to. And, lastly, the final idea is connected to our social skills, that'll identify the quality of the associations we enter into. This may be summarized as follows:

Lifestyle: Type or Quality of females you see.

Courage: Number of females you approach.

Social skills: Quality on the affair you start.

These 3 things are interrelated, along with collectively they function as a product. The 3 are happening in everybody's life, and everyone has their very own weaknesses and strengths. It's also visiting to look at males with good interpersonal skills but just for relating with the peers of theirs; this issue might get from getting little experience and contact with females during the childhood theirs. In other instances, one can see males that have a good degree of courage but bad sociable abilities. Although they're nerve adequate to address numerous females, they do not appear to have had some success in their attempts. We'll, consequently, analyze every concept in detail to subsequently see just how they perform concerning each other.

Lifestyle:

We might create life as to how a person decides to follow. It's connected to our tastes, addictions, values, and traditions. Additionally, it involves our socioeconomic status. For example:

● On a Saturday evening, do we fail and stay in and

observe a film?

● Do we purchase fine, expensive clothes, or perhaps we are always on the search for product sales?

● At what time selecting a spot for dinner, do we choose a stylish restaurant or maybe a diner?

● Do we wish to enjoy a peaceful life or even one filled with adventure?

● Do we picture a lifestyle with plenty of kids and do we prioritize professional business and development?

● Do we practice some sport? Do we chase some passion? Are we into visiting brand new places or perhaps do we prefer to sit down on our couch and remain on our own?

As it's been frequently stated before, individuals seem to get together with people who have a comparable lifestyle, that's, a method of coping with that they can identify; they're susceptible for getting together with people who talk about the same values, socioeconomic status, ideology, etc.

Allow me to exemplify: in case we have got an impressive socioeconomic status, next we are going to have far more risks to be with females with that same condition; in case we live with the parents of ours and also don't have any leads, we cannot count on to be using a professional design. If we're not famous at all, we cannot count on dating a movie star to date. If we're heavy and dress slovenly, we'll probably finish up with females that do the same. This has very little to do with the number of females we can connect with. A male belonging to a reduced social class, and with very little cash, might day thousands of females. Nevertheless, it's correct that creating a greater lifestyle typically is a door opener with regards to interacting.

In case we have a job we don't like, buddies we do not like, or maybe we're unemployed and do not direct the life we will wish to, we'll likely, besides, fail with females. Many questions could be available in handy to evaluate our situation: in case we might do anything we needed, totally free of limitations, and with no risks of disappointment, what would we do? Numerous women and men for that matter feel disappointed, and they're under the perception that their issue is just in their relationships when it derives from an absence of development in many aspects of their lives.

Courage:

Statistically, the higher the number of females we use, the better outcomes we are going to get and also the more females we'll be with. Naturally, our probability of doing well in each interaction will rely on the amount of the game of ours. For unique males, even if they've produced business dynasties, fought within the battle, applied intense sports, climbed mountains, and written novels, the simple sight of a female inside a sexy skirt is sufficient to build their hearts and minds quiver.

Approaching a female makes us uneasy due to our dread of rejection. The more our anxiety about becoming rejected, the greater anxiety we'll experience. Overall, the more nerve or courage we have, the less we are going to suffer the consequences of anxiety, since anxiety is usually chronic, regardless of whether it originates from our genes or maybe we get it from our environment. This could be the situation in case your dad endured social anxiety, as well as you learned to connect with others by watching his interactions. It might, besides, be a consequence of a trauma you've encountered. If being somewhat new, we fail to go to a pub and are therefore rejected in our very first seduction attempts, we may be damaged. Anxieties are by absolutely no sign fleeting, and almost everyone goes through some degree of anxiety, however mildly. It might be a mark we have with us for daily life, it might be natural to us. But relax: the reality is that we can muffle it right down to the stage where its effect is negligible. This way, we are going to be ready to create a good base of confidence in our capability to take care of a situation. In many instances, it's charming, to begin with, modest goals. For instance, in case you feel sick at ease with speaking with an attractive female, you can begin by approaching her and also simply asking her the moment. Therefore, as you develop much more comfortably, you are going to be ready to enhance your interactions. It's essential to have the ability to know when we're lying to ourselves or perhaps making excuses. When we're under a good amount of anxiety, our subconscious mind deploys a toolbox of defense mechanisms to rationalize our fears.

Has it never occurred to you that a reason you often resorted to unexpectedly becomes unimportant once you eventually decide to do everything you had been staying away from? In this case, what was the actual reason we had been earning the justification for ourselves? It is very simple: since we weren't being truthful with ourselves. Nowadays, most people will always be speaking about precisely how crucial it is to constantly appear happy, and just how everything must be fun: the publications we read, the films we view, the conversations we've had. If items aren't, then we're not "cool". It's like becoming furious is bad; we constantly need to think positive and also have an "it's-all-cool" mindset. The issue is the fact that we ought to acknowledge exactly how we truly feel; we should accept ourselves and begin the switch from there. We should not deny our feelings; we must foremost and first be truthful with ourselves. Lifestyle is a set of different emotions. It's flawlessly alright to always be angry; anger is an emotion also it's not bad, it's only a warning that food is happening with us. The issue isn't understanding why we're angry or continuing to be in that particular expression. If you're disgruntled plus you act like you're not, you'll most definitely become even angrier. If you concede the way you think rather than attempting to fight it and conceal it, it is going to be less difficult to feel better. The same transpires with fear. If we're scared, the greatest thing we can do is concede the circumstances and get it from there.

There's something comprehended as a "comfort zone," which happens to be a district where we think we're at solace. If we want something a lot more from our daily lives, then we are going to have to go and secure it. This will likely involve mental energy, actions, and motivation. If we're slothful, in that case, we'll barely develop some change. What would occur if we had taken the time we spend watching television or perhaps surfing the web and invested it in anything even more effective? It's about creating our self-worth. Individuals who believe they're in charge of their lives are likely to be more content. All those who feel helpless and therefore are scared of shifting on will likely regardless of the quantity of enjoyment of their life feel unpleasant for having remained within the old track. Developing courage is essential for any achievement of well-being, and also for conference females.

Interpersonal Skills:

Social abilities are differentiated by just how effectively you speak your emotions and intents, and also by the way you move other folks. The more you can enrich the interactions you're engaged in, the more long-lasting and pure they'll be. Interpersonal skills are directly associated with emotional intelligence. The most common mistakes are indicating emotional neediness and also investing over a female does, both before and also while in the relationship. Men who show signs of emotional neediness tend to mix up female authorization with attraction.

HOW TO SEDUCE WOMEN

TALK, ACT, AND LOOK LIKE A MAN

When it comes down to it, all approaches and all wider relations with women are about keeping your integrity as a man. That's it. It may sound simple, but this integrity should be manifest in every element of your presentation: how you dress, your stance, the tone of your voice, what you say, and your text messages, everything. Understand that they program women to select the highest value males they can reproduce with, and so they will constantly test you to ensure you fit the bill. Mostly, presenting your masculine self unapologetically and emphatically will make the difference between a successful approach and a blowout. Too many guys approach girls if they do it at all in a weak and wishy-washy manner. Cut that out right now. To be successful, you really need to go in there and own each interaction like a man.

Just how Soon to Approach

There used to be something called the three-second rule that was very popular in the seduction community. Basically, you would allow yourself only three seconds to talk to any girl you liked, as waiting any longer would give you more time to become nervous and bailout. The danger with this is that guys risk looking socially awkward by storming up to women indiscriminately. Women like to feel special, and that we have selected them for a reason. The danger with immediate approaches is that they give the lie to this impression. That said, walking right up to a girl off the bat communicates masculine confidence and that you are a guy who goes for what he wants, and these qualities are absolutely the key to attracting women. So don't tether yourself to a hard-and-fast timing rule, but approach and do the business as quickly as you can. You should keep a target in mind for how many women a day you will approach. It needn't be a high number, say ten on a night out at a club or one a day on your way to work. It doesn't matter as long as you've it in stick and mind to it. Ideally, however, you need to be racking up the figures and becoming the maximum amount of experience of talking to females under your belt as much as you can and also many new connections in your cellphone. As reported earlier, however, this is not just a numbers game. In addition, it's important that you guarantee that the quality of your method is high so you maximize your chances with every girl and each girl.

So how can this be achieved?

Fake It 'til You Make It: Now this, of course, is easier said than done, especially if you are not particularly self-confident and haven't been through years of social conditioning. Don't worry. It's hard for many of us at first, particularly in a climate that encourages self-effacement and permission seeking. The trick is simply to pretend. Fake it 'til you make it. What does this mean in practice? Go as much as the female pretending you believe you're the prize, feigning you feel it entitles you, pretending you're screening her, even when the truth is you believe she's extremely healthy for you. Squash some thoughts of inferiority hard. They're completely unhelpful as well as false. Objectively, you're both only human beings, along with nobody individual is "better" than the other person.

Your Approach Creates Attractions:

It's a secret that very few people - only those who cold-approach regularly know: your approach creates attraction in a woman. Earlier we discussed looks and height and their importance in meeting and attracting women, but the whole "looks" argument is a red herring. Yes, they help, and you need to have your fundamentals down, but if you approach like a man with confidence, then this boosts your perceived attractiveness. Put it this way: had my photograph been shown with those of several other men too many of the girls I've fucked or dated prior to our meeting, I'm fairly certain that they wouldn't have picked me out as being especially hot or great looking, but it's irrelevant. They became attracted to me because of my approach and the nature of our interaction. Yes, female mating decisions may be made within seconds, but it does not base them solely on physical criteria. Therefore, never wait for a sign of interest from a girl before approaching her. I've pulled girls who didn't so much as glance in my direction before I started talking to them and always take every opportunity that presents itself to you.

Chat:

The former portion of the discussion must comprise talking and maybe telling stories about yourself or maybe stuff you have experienced. These should not be boastful. The very last thing you should do is look as though you're attempting to wow, as this will come across as needy and it is unattractive, but aim to be like a great, interesting guy. Do not complain or even whine or bitch about anything. Keep a good vibe, but also do not act pleased with what she claims either. After 2 minutes, it is cool to drop by two issues being here to start about herself and also to supply you with much more material to work with, though you have to have provided some benefit first., you do not wish to seem like an interviewer, and precisely why must she respond to a barrage of concerns from someone she is only just met? After you have a typical talk with a female, it is beneficial to consider it to be a website's advertising strategy. Just keep on putting the information available until something prints heavy traffic or even in this situation a beneficial effect. Essentially, just keep on talking about anything you wish to until anything hits. Naturally, that begs the question: just where do you source your conversational material from? The actual solution to the question "What can I say" is the fact that you already know what you should say. When you look over this publication, it is safe to state you have more than a decade's worth of experiences that are unique, feelings, then images to talk about already. The issue that many people encounter is the fact that when meeting people that are new, we get stifled, and the conversation just does not arrive at us as.

Easily as it'd normally be. Just think about

how you will behave with a team of buddies when you 're. Calm and within the zone. The conversation flows from you, correct? You do not need primers to let you know what you should chat about and spend lots of your time considering what topics will impress you. You discuss whatever it's you wish to look at, and also in case it bombs, then you definitely do not strain and only open another thread. That's precisely what you have to get when you are conversing with that hot female. Walk up pretending you're the guy type that moves as he talks to females, and also it is much more probable that you'll be. And like anything, practice truly helps. Subjecting yourself to the art form just where spoken dexterity can be a prerequisite will benefit you. And remember you have a full lifetime's worth of content in your head. Believe that and allow it to go. Have confidence you will be ready to haul in the discussion. In the long run, the most effective way to get wonderful would be to approach as many females as you are able to. Probably the most helpful challenge you are able to set yourself as well as the one I have performed often is approaching a hundred females a month along with logging their reactions. If you want, capture several of these interactions so you are able to see exactly where you might do much better. Consistently placing yourself on the series this way does not merely cause you to produce exciting material to chat about, though additionally, it quickly explains the things that work and what do not and can enable you to to create your own personal working "script," a backbone for potential interaction which may be amended as needed when you see a new female.

Fear of Rejection: Understand that every person experiences this, and also it's completely natural. Additionally, it recognizes it's influenced by early fears dating right back to prehistoric times, the place that the rejection of a female intended ostracisation from the tribe as well as death. Nowadays, the most terrible event you're more likely to experience is a bit of mild embarrassment. In the great bulk of instances, so long as you've your basics down and therefore are non-threatening and presentable once you use a female, simply among 2 elements will happen:

- She will be flattered, show interest, and engage in a conversation that it is your job to advance.
- She will say, "Thanks, but I'm not interested" or "Thanks, but I have a boyfriend" or some variation of that.

In general, females like being approached still in case they're not into you, especially in the day when it seldom occurs. Mainly on extremely few occasions does something worse occur, really, and, so what can she do besides provide you with a dirty appearance and walk off and show you getting lost? If either of these items does occur, do not worry. You've accomplished nothing incorrectly. In the function that she does not happen to teach you charm, that's altogether her preference. You will attempt to learn and ease off, though it does not indicate you were not appropriate to converse with her in every situation. The point is the fact that rejection takes place all of the time in all aspects of life. It's simply one thing you have to recognize and also discover how to manage and get through to be able to attain anything. In reality, you ought to figure out how to like rejection, since whenever you get rejected, it indicates you're in the game and you're hustling, and that is infinitely better than flooring the sidelines plus watching.

Each successful seducer, just as each effective business person, craftsman, or sports person, has needed to encounter dismissal and difficulty to get to where they are today. This is essentially guaranteed. Any pickup craftsman or item that reveals to you is lying to bring in cash. Any man who has laid down an enormous number of ladies will have been dismissed by a ton progressively, similarly as the effective sales rep will have reached many a bigger number of possibilities than those he winds up changing over, however that doesn't make a difference. The end more than justifies the means. What you must do is start loving the process. Enjoy talking to different women and realize that each interaction that ends with a blowout is getting you closer to a yes; and just the fact that you approached in the first place puts you in the top 5 per cent of men, above all those others who you should view or wouldn't have dared to do so. Rejection in the same way regardless of how attractive the girl is. When a woman is hot, the stakes can seem higher, but when you think about it, it's a logical fallacy that her opinion counts for any more than a less-. In fact, her opinion holds no attractive person's greater worse than anyone else's, and it is hers alone. The next girl you speak to may well be into you. Such is the variegated nature of female desire. Never make the mistake of believing that anyone's opinion is universal; in fact, women have so many more criteria for sexual attraction than men do that their differences in taste are even rejections. Treat it as broader feedback. And so do not care about individuals in the approach of yours, adapt, and continue on. Just remember that the better you use, the happier you are going to get at doing these interactions as well as the more chances you produce on your own. And remember: nothing great in daily life ever comes easily.

YOUR DREAM DATE

Where to have her? What to chat about?

I firmly believe that if I really like a girl, then we will just need a good conversation to have a good time. For that reason, I always propose unfancied encounters. I generally ask them out for a drink in some pub. And this is my first piece of advice: to have a good time with a woman, you don't need anything grand; the main interest of the date must lie in meeting the other person. Considering ourselves a source of fun that interests her that's what's positive. Taking that as a basis, anything else one might want to add will be a plus, it will constitute further entertainment. I have always been amused by the importance an encounter can acquire simply by calling it a "date". Sometimes dates are held to be highly important and serious matters. But it's like giving a name to the way you meet with friends. It is better to think of it as something informal and casual as if we were just meeting a friend who is a girl. It is not a job interview or a university exam, you don't have to get a passing mark. We are there to have fun with someone. Not every day is the same. People often make plans for the weekend, so Friday and Saturday may not be the best choices to go out with a girl we have just met. Monday is also usually not a good choice since it is the beginning of the week and it tends to be a tiring day. The way I see it, Tuesdays, Wednesdays, Thursdays and Sundays are as good of days as any to go out with someone. I recommend scheduling the encounter for the afternoon or the evening. This allows for greater intimacy and gives the encounter a more sensuous atmosphere.

Where to take her?

I believe the proper question is "What do we enjoy doing?" We should select areas regarding our lifestyle or maybe the stuff we love. We should not attempt to impress her with something expensive and out of reach of us. There's no promise of success. Heading to the films is among the most timeless options, but not among the greatest since it does not provide you with the chance to speak and be familiar with one another.

The same happens with going out for dinner, it doesn't leave space for creating sexual intimacy. I believe there are places which allow for greater opportunities. For the sake of convenience and logistics, it is also a good idea to pick a venue relatively close to home. If we're twenty kilometers away, it might be hard to get her back to our place. If our place is not a possibility, then it is probably a good idea to check beforehand whether there are hotels. It is said that our level of intimacy with others comes from the number of shared experiences. Keeping this principle in mind, we can generate greater affinity with someone if we interact with them in various places, instead of just one. It is advisable to visit two or three different places, although moving across long distances may make us both tired. Consider also how many emotions or experiences you can generate in the encounter. This is what I call an "emotional roller coaster". It is always a good idea to take an interest in the other person, to talk about our passions or other deep issues. She might mean a lot to us, but she is still only human, so let's not regard her as our one true love. In all probability she is not. We might both be nervous: we met last night at a party and now we are sitting quietly in an ice-cream place. That's just normal. If silences are to come up, it's best to accept them as something natural; they are not a bad thing. We should try to think of her as someone we have known for a long time: there is no need to plan what we are going to talk about, or what we are going to do, or what the best mechanisms to make her feel comfortable are. Those things simply happen. If we are curious about meeting new people, then it will be difficult for us not to find something in common with the other person, especially if we are there sitting side by side.

What to chat about?

Speaking to females is a lot different from speaking with the buddies of yours. To get great at it, you will need to focus on the skills of yours by practicing. With females, there can be occasions when you simply click, and also interaction is outstanding between the 2 of you. You do not have to worry about what you should say next, plus you are found in a great conversation. On the other hand, there can be occasions when you encounter terrible cessation and do not understand what to mumble. What is the goal of interaction between the 2 individuals all things considered? The primary objective is usually to become familiar with one another better. To obtain an approximate opinion of each other 's view and personality of the planet. To find out in case you press for on well. Aside from this, females will question themselves about the feelings of theirs or maybe the approach they think about you after speaking with you.

I am certain you would like the date of you to enjoy and also you wish to have fun, also! We would like to make sure that the conversation interests both individuals. Body language speaks first in every discussion. When you're tight or not at simplicity with yourself, you will sit back, crossing your legs, maybe your arms, your mouth will barely break a smile, and your eyes will search elsewhere in space. Knowing this can enable you to impart trust with your body language. Your verbal dating conversation abilities will mostly be gauged on just how able you are to create a conversation your partner enjoys. Ultimately, which results in you getting far more dates. If you think this's apparent, it is! The issue is how you can develop a fascinating discussion. We will keep up with individuals both answering and asking questions. If you question the questions, your partner will have fun. If you question the wrong questions, they'll ditch you. If you're less evasive than sincere when responding to her questions, she'll ditch you quicker.

Here are a few conversation starter question ideas covering your very first date:

"What do you like doing in your emergency time?"

"What do you especially like about that?"

"If you could go for an illusion vacation, someplace on the planet, in which would it be and what might you do?"

By asking these inquiries, you will be ready to remember enjoyable experiences and also share them along with you. Phases of every male-female interaction move through. You can speed up the process, though you cannot bypass some phases.

1. The very first detail is loosening up somewhat in each other's business. You can discuss superficial topics; it does not matter. People require some time to allow themselves to loosen up some, getting used to the planet and the other person, particularly on a day.

2. At the stage when you are slackened up, the

subsequent phase is accomplishing an affinity with each other. Discovering shared traits, points and regular interests in which it connects you 2 is fundamental.

3. When you've affirmed typical passions, you can focus on establishing trust and comfort. A female want to find out if she can believe in you before giving her body to you. She needs to realize that you will not harm her physically or even escape her right after having sex. For ages, females who lost their chastity before it labelled them matrimony sluts and pushed them to the edges of society. Nowadays, it is a group superior, but females continue to ponder the way their friends will react. Society continues to place an impressive deal of stress on them. That is the reason this stage is very essential.

4. The quarter stage is also her arousal. The very first 3 phases will relatively safeguard that during the procedure of arousal, cultural training will not kick in. Each point provided above is within a

cause-and-effect connection with the future one. Having sex with her arouses her. You are able to quickly arouse her but to avoid social conditioning via kicking in, she will need to believe in you. But trust will come just after the connection, and also rapport is after loosening up. See? It's like creating a home. If you bypass the foundation or even simply take strides, your house will quickly collapse. Going through all 4 phases is necessary.

JUST HOW AND WHEN WE SHOULD KISS A GIRL

The term "kino" comes from NLP (Neuro-Linguistic Programming) and it refers to physical contact, touching, and being touched. Physical contact is an element of non-verbal communication. During the process of seduction, putting kino into practice has a double effect: for one, when we touch a woman, the sexual temperature rises. At the same time, it creates emotional tension, which translates in her having a greater disposition to listen to us and be invested in us. It is important not to touch someone when it is out of place, and to avoid looking like a stalker. In short, we should take care not to invade the other's space. We also must take into account the local customs: there are countries in which physical contact is less frequent. In that respect, we must take in the concept of "kino escalation". In other words, if she is uncomfortable with taking us by the hand, we cannot expect her to be comfortable with kissing us. Kino escalation helps us advance progressively. A good example of a failed kino escalation can be seen in dates, where, because the man is "too much of a gentleman" and overly "respects" the woman, the kino escalation is not initiated at the right time, so they try to kiss at the last minute, which ultimately feels forced and uncomfortable. What usually transpires when a man fails to touch a woman at the proper period is that, as the interaction progress, it becomes increasingly difficult to establish a physical connection, and the distance between them widens. For this reason, physical contact should escalate progressively, but from the very beginning. The most significant thing is to feel pleased touching others in such a way that our conversations will be improved. But fair warning: touching girls willy-nilly, just like telling jokes nonstop, will get you nowhere. It is just one aspect to be taken into account when trying to create chemistry and move forward with a woman.

Kino must be used in a way that is subtle but also expresses firmness and dominance. It can be divided into accidental or intentional contact.

Accidental contact gets that name because the idea is that it goes unnoticed, it has the aim of subconsciously increasing communication and trust between the two parties, generally when they have just met. This commonly involves arms, elbows, hands, etc. Intentional contact is much more explicit; it aims to express interest in a much more direct way. This could be done by hugging her, grabbing her, caressing her, touching her leg, etc. This generally takes place between people who already know each other, or in situations with a more relaxed and informal atmosphere. For example, when dancing with a woman we may establish accidental or intentional contact depending on what we want to bring into focus. We may use dancing as an excuse to establish physical contact, not making a point of the fact that we are touching. Or we might make it intentional, emphasizing the actual touching, rather than the dancing. We may employ either one as a means to communicate.

Kissing is a way to create and also communicate bonding and affection, and that fosters a sensation of peacefulness together with the other's company. Kissing is part of the kino escalation. We do not have to request anything or permission from here. I've kissed females under many conditions which I will say the proper method to get it done is...to just get it done. The solely related sign is that she's there alongside us and is also paying attention to our conversation for over 15 minutes...or maybe 5 hours! She would like to undertake it. Or even as it's typically said: in case we feel she needs us to kiss her, next she most likely wants it for some time.

An amazing technique to achieve the kiss is, to be honest: try saying something like "I'd like to kiss you" or "I'm so nervous, but I want to kiss you". We may get nervous, feel paralyzed, or uncomfortable, or maybe we just cannot see how we can move forward. We may get the feeling that she is not like other girls and that we should wait. These kinds of things have happened to everyone at one point or another. The point is to try it, to go for it. If she turns her head or says no, then we apologize, say sorry, or smile. But I feel certain it is better to fail than be left with the doubt of whether we could have accomplished it. Some girls don't kiss in public places or around their friends. Some never kiss in nightclubs or on first dates. Better try again somewhere more private. Being an excellent kisser may play a fundamental part in getting called back by women. All jokes aside, we may have struck her as an exceptional guy, but if she didn't enjoy kissing us, we may never see her again. Lastly, we ought to show some restraint and, if interested in seeing her again, not advance too much the first few times around. That could cause something commonly known as "buyer's remorse": if a woman advances overly fast in sexual terms, immediately satisfying her feelings of attraction, she may regret it later. This is the same thing that happens when we buy something on a whim and then realize we didn't need it.

Kissing is a vital step. In reality, not doing it might make her lose interest and also get neutral. Though we should remember it's a component of the trip, not the ultimate location. The best and simplest technique to get her number We've met an incredible female, maybe we kissed her (or perhaps not), and also we'd love to see her once again. We move to request her phone number or maybe her Facebook (or perhaps some other interpersonal network) address. If she's interested in us, she will give it to us while not beating all around the bush. From my experience, it's best never to provide it with a lot of thought or even attempt to earn several complicated excuses: it's only requesting the number of her and also providing her with ours. There's absolutely nothing to hide. The one thing which nearly all problems and scares males is getting a fake telephone number, to not be called again, and that later on, she shows minimal interest. Though the issue is not in just how we requested her number, but in what our conversation with her was like. If she's not into us, it may be a lot easier for her to simply give us her number and after that not respond to our calls. At any rate, it's more beneficial never to go to conclusions. Possibly she's keen on us but couldn't answer the telephone for several specific reasons. She might have been returning home and also had a crash, she might have lost her phone, perhaps she met another guy or perhaps she was not prepared to head out with someone new. Perhaps she didn't wish to see us. You can turn it out to anyone.

Additionally, males are usually experienced with concerns like as "When must I phone her?", "How long must I wait around answering her messages?", "How must I consult her out?" Many folks impose rules on themselves, like not making some communication for a week, or to draw exactly two times time she did to reply to. This may be counterproductive. All of it boils down to if she's into us. If she had been madly into us, will she say "I cannot do tomorrow, I mentioned I'd shop with a friend"? Absolutely no means! She will question the friend of her for a rainfall check which will fix the issue.

What's the greatest moment to kiss a female?

Kissing is a way to create and also communicate bonding and affection, and that fosters a sensation of peacefulness together with the other 's company. Kissing is part of the kino escalation. We do not have to request her anything or permission else. I've kissed females in many conditions which I will say the proper method to get it done is…to just get it done. The solely related sign is she's there alongside us, and also is paying attention to us talk for more than 15 minutes…or maybe 5 hours! She possibly would like to undertake it. Or even as it's typically said: in case we feel she needs us to kiss her, next she most likely is wanting it for some time. An amazing method to get the kiss is, being honest: try saying a thing as "I'd love to kiss you" or maybe "I'm anxious, though I wish to kiss you". We might get nervous, or uncomfortable, feel paralyzed, and perhaps we simply can't determine exactly how we can move ahead. We could get the sense that she's not like some other females which we ought to hold out. These types of things have happened to every person at some point or perhaps some other. The thing is giving it a shot, going for it. In case she turns the head of her or even says no, subsequently we apologize, mention sorry, or just laugh. Though I feel sure it's far better to go wrong than remain with the question of whether we might have achieved it.

Some females do not kiss in places that are public or perhaps around the friends of theirs. Some in no way kiss of nightclubs or on first dates. To be a great kisser might play a fundamental component in getting called again by females. Finally, we must show a little restraint and, in case interested in seeing her once again, not advance a lot of the very first couple of times around. This might lead to something commonly acknowledged as "buyer's remorse": so long as a female advance extremely quick in sexual terminology, right away fulfilling the feelings of her of attraction, she could regret it later. This's the same that occurs when we purchase anything on a whim, after which understand we did not require it.

Kissing is a vital step, in reality, not doing it might make her lose interest and also get neutral. Though we should remember it's a component of the trip, not the ultimate location. The best and simple technique to get the number of her We've met an incredible female, maybe we kissed her (or perhaps not), and also we'd love to see her once again. We move, then, to request the phone number of her or maybe the Facebook of her (or perhaps some other interpersonal network) address. In case she's interested in us, she is going to give it to us while not beating all around the bush. From the experience of mine, it's best never to provide it with a lot of thought or even attempt to earn several complicated excuses: it's only a question of requesting the number of her and also providing her ours. There's absolutely nothing to hide. The one thing which nearly all problems and scares males is the idea of obtaining a fake telephone number, to not be called again, and that later on, she shows minimal interest. Though the issue is not in just how we request the number of her, but in what the conversation of ours with her was like. In case she's not into us, it may be a lot easier for her to simply give us the number of her and after that not respond to the calls of ours. At any rate, it's more beneficial never to go to the conclusions. Possibly she's keen on us but wasn't in the position to answer the telephone for a number of a specific reason. She might have been returning home and also had a crash, she might have lost the phone of her, perhaps she met another guy or perhaps she was not prepared to head out with someone new. All those things occur all of the time, and also it's not worth curious about what might have occurred. Perhaps she didn't wish to see us it can happen to anybody.

Also, males are usually experienced with concerns such as: "When must I phone her?", "How long must I wait around answering her messages?", "How must I consult her out?" Many folks impose on themselves rules including not making some communication for a week, or to draw exactly two times the time she did to reply to. This may be counterproductive. The fact is the fact that it all boils down to whether she's into us or perhaps not. Think of it this particular way: we're a crucial famous person and we ask her out. No means!

SEXUALIZE THE INTERACTIONS OF YOURS WITH WOMEN

At no point ought there be some anxiety that you're identifying with one another in every capacity apart from a male lady. This standard format, albeit unwritten, is unshakeable and resolute and also applies in most instances. Ladies possess a binary sexual strategy: they search for alpha "lovers" to have sex with and also to impregnate them, and so they look for beta "provider" kinds to take care of them and raise their children. Today most females will refute this, and people almost all have various agendas, though you can see this pattern played out all the time. First, place yourself in an alpha camp. Even if you're a beta provider who wishes nothing much more than to settle down as the woman of her dreams in cozy household circumstances, to make it happen, you have to first attract the female.

After sex, when you've decided you like her and also you should get into a relationship with her, it's somewhat simple to turn down a gear to beta, though it's difficult going the opposite way. Sex cements the attraction between you and also makes it unequivocal that this is a male woman dynamic. Absolutely nothing else matters as an appropriate response to a strategy, not flirtation, not kissing. In the present-day sexual marketplace, these items are meaningless. A female will not consider you as being a serious proposition till right after she has slept with you (and never next, sometimes).

HOW TO SEDUCE WOMEN

SEX AND CRITICAL TOPICS

Once she's loosened up in your company and you also have a satisfying relief, trust, and connection with her, you can shift the conversation toward sexual guidance so she'll be well prepared for the very first kiss. The subject of sex is something you can never, ever be immediate about. You cannot ask a female: "Do you wish to have sex with me?" while in case you think she does. There's a game which I love. It is kind of like an icebreaker just for the very first day. It provides a framework for each individual to ask questions you would not ordinarily wonder about over a very first day and also brings up the subject of sex. Do not take it seriously; it just works whether you get it done delightfully and funnily. It's not really a game to relax in when things are uncomfortable. Get it in place if each of yours LOOSENED Up and also Feeling GOOD. Tell her to find an interesting and entertaining game you wish to show her. And also the previous rule: She surely goes first. She will not have the choice to question anything and can pass the ball to your court. Listed here are a couple She will not have the choice to question anything and can pass the ball to the court of yours.

Listed here are a few explorations you can pose. Notice just how they direct her a sexual way:

1. Questions about earlier associations - ideal for a start: Exactly how many boyfriends do you have?

2. At what moment did you have your initial boyfriend?

3. Inquiries regarding sex - ideal for stirring her and leading to her to think about the subject; to find out whether she seems to be okay with it

4. What did you choose the most, and what did you detest most likely the most about him?

5. What was missing in your relationship with your final boyfriend?

6. What was missing in your relationships with your boyfriends of up to today?

7. Do you need excitement, passion, adventure, and

therefore are you a romantic individual?

8. Have you been within love?

9. Which one of your boyfriends did you such as the many?

10. What was the most fantastic place that you invested in a period with him?

11. With your prospective boyfriend, what's probably the most wonderful place to spend time in?

12. What's possibly the craziest thing you've finished in a relationship and even for love?

2. Themes regarding kissing will take her picture to the point:

13. When did you last kiss a person?

14. When did you have your total first kiss?

15. At what time did you have the main kiss that you truly appreciated? Show what it really resembled.

16. Did you earlier kiss a guy over the initial day? Just so how did it happen?

17. Describe your perfect kiss - what it's like!

18. What was the most thrilling appliance you did when playing "truth or dare"?

19. If you were to identify between sex and friendship in a relationship with a fellow, what kind might you choose?

20. Have you at any time had one evening rendezvous?

21. Have you at any time involved in sexual relations on the key date?

22. Just how frequently do you indulge in sexual relations when you're seeing someone?

23. Where is probably the strangest area you at any time involved in sexual relations?

24. Have you at any point involved in sexual relations in wide daylight?

25. What is your preferred place?

26. At what time did you take part in sexual relations only because?

27. Have you at any time experienced a trio with another little woman or even fellow?

28. Okay, attempt it?

29. What is probably the most outrageous item you have completed while partaking in sexual relations?

30. What was lacking inside your sexual coexistence around today?

31. Do you masturbate? How frequently?

32. Describe what ultimate sex is very much love for you.

I cannot stress enough to evaluate the responses of her and calibrate. On the out chance that she is not pleased with the greater sexual subject matter, do not constrain it. It is going to differ from a young person to a young woman. On the out chance that she is a virgin, she might blush if you present a percentage of the very first inquiries. In case she seems to be tough, change the design. Ask something much less interesting and ignore the whole game.

The game is amazing for gauging what type of girl she is. After participating in it, you will decide whether she's a down or romantic more - earth individual, whether she requires sex as a regular item or maybe she's much more of a conventional style, etc. With this info, you can customize your style to her personality. If she's a hot female, she will be much more ready to accept developing maybe and physically having sex on the very first day. If she's romantic, you can take your time and let her be much more comfortable in your company by awaiting several additional dates. If everything goes well throughout the game, note the signals she's driving via her body language. It may prepare her to be kissed after many more sexual questions and even a kiss. Watch for the peak stage of your conversation when her pupils dilate, and her breath quickens. That is the use of choosing for the kiss.

SEXUAL TENSION

The capacity to set up sexual tension and sit in it easily is a significant contrast between a dexterously attractive man who gets fast outcomes, and a bumbling over-active supplicatory who goes out of his way at every point to make the woman feel ok, glad and satisfied at all times, never wanting to step on her toes. This is the typical crutch of the friendly guy who feels he has to be super nice and overly accommodating to earn a woman's attraction. Most guys you see interacting with women will do one of the following things to absolutely KILL any chance of sexual tension and releasing pressure continuously. i.e. - getting in his way.

• Nodding at everything she says like an over-eager horse

• Over the top smile was unnecessary

• Laughing at absolutely nothing

• Breaking eye contact/not holding

• Moving/fidgeting

• Speaking quickly

• Carrying the entire conversation because he does not allow her space to talk.

The above are the principal areas that you can get out of right now and see happening straight away. I bet while reading through that list, many of them will sound familiar to your interactions. Well, this is good, because now you have an awareness of it. With practice, you can shed these overtly accommodating and weak traits. When you ask her a question in a slow relaxed and sexy manner, allow her to answer, fully. Do not jump in, do not offer a remedy, do not move onto your next factual question. Allow her to delve and to fill the silence. And how do you do that? Give her silence. Also, when you are looking at her speak, look directly into her left eye, and feel her. Feel her wrapped around your penis. Enjoy it, it's a certainty. She will feel this, and the interconnection of both energies will very surprise you. Be aware of how she blushes, breaks eye contact, and giggles for absolutely no reason. When she finishes her sentence, allow a second or two space from her. This will do two exceptional things. Creating tremendous amounts of sexual tension makes HER work for you, not the other way around. By not being as reactive to her amazing heart as all the other overly eager guys, this will instantly intrigue her. "Why the hell is he not jumping through hoops to get me? Ah, maybe this guy is unique. Maybe this is the man who can give what I desire" I have had gorgeous girls ask me "Hey, why are you not trying to get me? Do you even like me?" then starting the kiss because they could not handle any more tension I was placing on them. It's a sexual tension bubble, where your environment and surroundings disappear, and you are both sitting in this sexually charged and bubbling bit of sexual energy. It is powerful! Be clear that this is NOT a technique... but an adaption of your behaviour to align yourself with your new understanding of sexual polarization. An understanding of how masculine and feminine interact with their opposites. Being socially correct will not get her into bed, being polarizing within your masculine core will...fast!

JUST HOW LONG WILL IT TAKE LAYING HER?

It's a question you may usually wonder about: How lengthy will it take to lay a female? The solution is: It relies on each of you: whether you are ready to begin properly and if it prepares her for it. When you ask friends of yours or maybe other men, several of them will say it has taken many weeks to place their girlfriends; many will state they laid her the very first night and over the 1st day. You've got a considerable level of influence over this, but installing a female who's a complete virgin and has never ever been kissed will call for a minor effort. Nearly all females will have absolutely no challenges having sex on two dates or perhaps on the very first day in case they love you. All those that demand extra labor fit into 3 categories: They're inexperienced, very, dealing with issues or even playing with you. Laying a virgin will call for an impressive deal of persistence. She will want to feel special along with you and also know you are concerned about her, like her, and will not escape her right after having sex. Teenage virgins are typically idealistic and think love is true. They quickly get emotionally connected to the guy that does it. When you do not love her and are considering going on before long, you must provide her before the action, unless she's an older virgin, in what situation she falls into the next class.

These are females with problems: those that haven't had an orgasm, whose initial sexual encounter was horrible, who have been raped and with severe inhibitions, perhaps because of their religious upbringing or even earlier sexual encounters. These females might be in an additional group, however, and want you to be equally thoughtful and conscientious as with virgins. They overcome their inhibitions with patience and love, and also after that, they are going to open up sexually. Such females can provide you with an impressive deal of love, and they're not females you've sex with then work on a different female. The 3rd category contains females with rules for acting difficult to get just playing with guys. Several of these females are warm with big egos and attitudes. They need and also enjoy sex, though they like it when males battle for them. You will listen to excuses from these females, like: "I'm not prepared for sex yet" or maybe "I do not feel special yet." The 3rd category contains females with rules for acting difficult to get just playing with guys. Several of these females are extremely warm with big egos and attitudes. They need and also enjoy sex, though additionally, they like it when males battle for them. You will listen to excuses from these females, like as: "I'm not prepared for sex yet" or maybe "I do not feel special yet."

Don't try to rape her, obviously, but become

more physical. These females have to find out just how effective you're. Show her you have choices, plus you're prepared to go on whenever. She must understand you're the selector, and also she's not in a place to help make the rules. You ought to function like the one in control and charge. Inform her you're not ready to accept playing the little games of her, and also she can often provide in or maybe you will move on fast. Ensure you never set unreachable goals on your own. In case you would like to place each chick on the very first day, it will not happen. With every single female you are dating, you must determine whether you would like a long-term relationship or maybe you are only just enjoying themselves with one another. If you love her personality and she appears to be the most perfect partner, it may well be worth waiting around some time even in case she's sexual inhibitions to get over. If you attempt to make things and also strike her aggressively, you may discourage a normally terrific female from being at bay. Naturally, with experience, you can sense the distance you can opt for a particular female. Consistently see through her game and, in case you believe she is playing you, go on. Never hold out for many weeks to place a female who is not well worth your time. Plus, even if a female demands an impressive deal of work, you need not devote yourself to her, and also you can see different females in the same period. Never restrict yourself or perhaps your opportunities. At what time does a relationship begin? I usually think a relationship has started after we have had sex. Hanging or kissing out together is nothing specific for many females, and also you must get it the same way. At least further up towards the use associated with sex, I consider it open, and I am seeing other females. It is about having choices. Why dedicate yourself to a female who will rarely have sex with you?

THE BEST WAY TO READ WOMEN: SIGNS THAT SHE'S ALL SET TO GO PHYSICAL

Normally, there's a unique power operating in male-female relationships. While females follow a passive, open demeanour, guys are a lot more energetic and initiative. A common instance in a club is a female's plan being approached, while men are more likely to approach girls. A female can do 2 items to improve her success: She can appear her greatest, skirt in high heels, etc., push-up bras, and she can also provide inviting clues for a guy to approach her. A guy will be much more likely to address a female that looks great in his eyes, though he'll also aim for a less hot one in case she shows symptoms of fascination and he views the green light. Along with these collections, in an average male-female connection, the female will flag with the non-verbal communication and also conduct that she's ready to keep on, even though the man will respond to her advance, align, and signs as requirements are. He must experience the means and begin, as she expects he must. By and also by, this's linked in with driving. It doesn't matter how amazing a conversationalist you are and regardless of the way it's pulled in for you, you'll constantly function as the one starting. Some horny and forceful women will do it for you, however, that's a unique situation without the standard format.

There are two types of female signs: subliminal and cognizant ones. A little woman will give cognizant signs when she wants you to create a turn of yours. Subliminal signs are subtler and can be a programmed response to her wonderfulness in your organization. It's crucial to become acquainted with these symptoms. By determining how you perceive the symptoms women are driving, you will improve your prosperity exponentially. In a club or even regular ordinary conditions, there'll regularly be a few youthful women around you presenting indications of intrigue and inviting you to move toward them using non-verbal communication. If you look at these youthful women and also make their turn, you'll most likely succeed.

And so let us look at the basic consciousness along with subconscious indications that show she's drawn to you:

1. She is calm while sitting and talking with you. Her arms are opened and never closed; her thighs and legs are sometimes wide apart or even crossed with her foot pointing toward you.

2. She's confident with the company of yours. When you lean nearer to her, she remains in a similar place and does not move out.

3. She leans closer while speaking with you or perhaps sits closer when you are sitting alongside one another.

4. She laughs a lot, laughing in the course of your lamest jokes, or perhaps she compliments you on a thing unremarkable.

5. She contacts you occasionally on your shoulder or arms when speaking with you.

6. She fixes the clothes of her, applies more makeup in the restroom, and actually exposes places of the body of her, revealing skin as well as showing erotic areas of her body.

7. She rubs the wrists of her up and down, plus rubs touch or strokes her cheeks.

8. She plays with the hair of her, pushing the fingers of her through it or twirling a couple of curls within sluggish, sensual actions.

9. She seems deep in the eyes of yours while grinning, her pupils dilated. She blinks faster than

regular or perhaps actually helps to keep entering the eyes of yours in a longing function, as the dog of yours when you're planning to feed him.

10. At this stage when you communicate with her and set your arms around her, she is OK with it; she might even cuddle closer to you.

11. At this stage whenever you stretch out the hand of yours to her, she calls for it and also holds it as although you are, as of today, a couple.

12. She nibbles the lips of her and licks them, giving the tongue of her, or perhaps she soaks the mouth of her with lipstick. If she places a finger or perhaps a nail in the mouth of her or even perhaps over it within sexually, these are indications of sexual musings, and they are typical indications of excitement. Just the way she sits and stands mirrors your nonverbal communication; she is reflecting on you.

She can't be doing everything at the very same time. Nevertheless, in case you've a lot more than a number of them (particularly the far more authentic ones), she is more than likely going to get very pulled in for yourself and also need you. An expression of caution: Just as you are going to find bashful individuals, you'll see similarly timid little ladies. They might earn some harder memories giving indications of intrigue and actively play along with you. They might furthermore try to conceal these signs. You are going to remember them from their innocent chaos.

Here are a few bad nonverbal communications, which shows an absence of engagement as well as less fascination within you: one. She looks away and converts away if you attempt to enjoy the eyes of her.

1. She frowns, indicating she's tired.

2. There's a very long, cumbersome hush in the discussion of yours, and she does not show some enthusiasm for separating the quietness or even bringing some new themes.

3. The legs of her as well as arms are crossed; she's sitting in a distance, or maybe she converts away from you. She leans back, and once you lean closer, she moves just or away functions as in case she is uncomfortable.

4. She does not respond to the jokes of yours and also does not laugh with you; she might exhibit polite surprise.

Furthermore, the rundown moves on. Although determination is a great characteristic to possess and again and now if it is persistent, you can recuperate from probably the saddest conditions, the bad clues portrayed above show that you have achieved something incorrectly, and yes it might be the ideal chance to move onward and scan for another little woman. Never be frustrated; accomplishment is going to accompany time and assurance.

THE MAKE-OUT

A good make-out meeting after kissing often leads promptly to sex. Picture you've kissed lately. Do things gradually, rushing nothing at many, and also brow heavy at her at whatever phase you are able to. Begin by operating your fingertips through the fur of her. Play with it, wrapping 2 blocks around the fingers of yours. You are able to furthermore grab a lock of the hair of yours and bring it softly. Smell her hair, neck, and shoulders some whether you have accomplished it already or not. Take deep, long breaths, as if you're breathing in air which is new. Let the nose of yours and also mouth contact these locations when smelling them.

After a while, start by softly kissing her neck and shoulders. Slowly advance up with her experience until you switch up at her mouth. This makes the female really want the kisses of yours a lot more. When you've established lots of fear, kiss her passionately for a while: Softly slide your tongue to her jaws, and permit it to stroll around. This is an erotic place for females. They love it in case you stroke and in addition caress it. You can get away from her locks and also smell the nape. This will probably drive her insane. Switch back and forth between smelling, brief kisses all over and neck, then profoundly suggestive individuals most of the rage. Only a few women in this manner type all around their ears, however. Gnawing her delicately in places is an impressive product for excitement. Start with her neck and shoulders first. There is a sexual location on her arms where her lower arms and also top-rated arms meet. Suggestive sucking and licking about the neck of her arms, shoulders, tits, along with; thighs will market to her also; don't drool.   While executing a portion of the abovementioned, allow your fingertips meander around the rear of her along with midriff region. At that moment contact the gut of her, belly, combined with the sides of the paper on the body of her; stroke as well as returned run them delicately. Perceive precisely how she responds. If she is uncertain, make a number of strides back; at that time advance steadily once more. Blend it up now and then: much like a touch of kissing, inside that particular moment gnawing, thus on., while stroking her with all the hands and wrists you have.

When you feel she is ready, steadily move on toward her far more sexual areas. Just in case she's at ease with this particular, escalate your touches: Start by carefully caressing her tits as well as the ass of her. Draw reducing hovers with your fingers and tongue on the bosoms of her via the outside to within that hope is able to make her insane. At that moment, snatch her tits a bit more generally and also brings her areolas. You are able to make use of licking, sucking, as well as gnawing to search for various vulnerable places on the entire body of her too.

Try not to disregard the rear end of her, legs, and also thighs. Back run them and allow your fingers to explore these zones. She might value delicate squeezes on the rear end of her. You can also bring a stab at punishing the rear end of her on more than a single occasion within a delicate however sexual fashion. Regardless if she likes additionally grounded or maybe less heavy connections will differ from little person to young woman. Investigation while producing away and also perceive exactly how she responds. On the outside likelihood that she wants it, stick with it. But you will find certain sexual zones that could be the equivalent for all those little females, each and every one will have a certain portion of her entire body that is touchier when compared with the others. Massage the pussy of her throughout the dresses of her. Slowly slide your hands inside the massage of her and also trousers the clitoris of her. Just in case she enables you to get it completed, set your fingertips within the panties of her, as well play with her empty pussy.

During the make out, she could point out conditions like: "We should not be performing this." "It's way too quickly for me." This's the rational component of the brain of her (social conditioning) kicking within. Unless she is upset, pulls out, or maybe tries to avoid you, simply ignore these comments. In case you persist in providing her the sensations as well as arousal that's needed, the animal instincts of her will take command, and also she'll be all set for sex. In case she stops you, stops right away! Do not force something, and also don't rape her! She may require a little while and also maybe all set by the following time you encounter. As I pointed out earlier, several females are going to require more hours than others.

HER PLACE OR PERHAPS YOURS

In case kissing or perhaps making out happens on the date of yours or perhaps at a club, it is intelligent attention to modify settings. A swarmed cafe possibly will not be the very best area for having intercourse. Simply expose to her you're burnt out on resting and state, "We must have a stroll!" Only at that stage, you've many options. In case you believe she is not yet prepared, achieve different things like going for a stroll within the leisure facility. In case she's ready, you will find usually 3 spots to go: the place of her, the place of yours, so the automobile. Okay, you can get it done within the bushes in the recreation center, however, that sometimes occurs. ☺ Let us look at each in detail:

1. **Her Abode:** This is just a chance in case she lives alone, or maybe you realize that her parents haven't been home for some time. After the day, you can provide to walk to her home or even take her by automobile. In case you go by automobile, park it near her apartment in a location in which you can make it for some time. Start kissing her goodbye, but also perform on arousing her. Follow the make out manual from chapter 4.8. Meanwhile, she may point out having to

keep or even being forced to get up at the start of the early morning these are only her rational brain's excuses, that show she's becoming far too aroused. If this occurs, gently but confidently drag the back of her and continue arousing her all the more.

Don't be assertive and don't rape her! Her body should show the symptoms she requires of you. If you've got to replicate the process in 4 events, do it four times. If you're fingering her pussy, although she still hasn't invited you inside, you will need to begin it. Question her if she really wants to invite you for only a cup of coffee or tea. Or just tell her you have got to work with her within the bathroom. At home, I remain and talk down. Experiment with allowing her to get at ease with your presence at her place. Slowly we start kissing and making out. Make sure you have a condom with you in your wallet, therefore there will be fewer "technical problems." Only then is sex likely to happen. If she doesn't want to supply it in, don't drive it. Experiment with giving her a bit of time; you have used most likely the most crucial matters and also could be close to installing her at a different time.

2. **Your Abode:** If she lives together with the parents, this is a single choice aside from having sex within the automobile. I typically wait for a date or even 2 before attractive her off to my place. As a basic guideline, always kiss and also create somewhat prior to attracting a female to go home with you and even store at her place! Just how soon you can invite her depends on the female you are working with. If you're knowledgeable, she's more than likely a virgin; it's useless to rush things. But in case they kiss themselves together, if she is like a sexy female, plus additionally in case you have in the past had the kiss, then aim for it. The easiest method is telling her you have a great recipe and you want to get ready for

her. Just in case you can't cook, offer to go shopping; likewise, prepare meals with her help. And explain to her you will purchase pizza and in addition have just a little fun together. If she's reluctant about approaching much more than even with several from you, then she's not ready for it. Hold on for many additional dates and in addition, help make your offer then at a later time.

Another way to do it is going away to the city to welcome her over. Try sitting at a cafe near yours and attend a close-by park for a stroll. Having something at home that will fill in as a goal is driving her to occur over. It is the uncommon music CDs of yours, DVD assortment, pictures you had taken during your movements, an ordinary intrigue you provide, and whatever else. Present the notion on your date, then offer to pass it on to her later: "I got my hands on that bizarre U2 compilation we talked about.

I live all around the bend. You can come over, and also we will audibly hear it out together." Do not be very dynamic, since she will identify the uncertainty of yours. Be coolly specific.

Set the frame of mind before she arrives. Light two torches and freeze some liquor or champagne in the fridge. You can likewise put on several relieving, quieting, tempting background sounds. At the point when she appears, kiss her with the entryway. Move her to the front apartment and speak a piece. She wants to get acquainted with the world and relax up somewhat. You can do some interesting things to go over in your footstool, for instance, a sculpture from your most recently available excursion to Africa or maybe a guide to sexual positions or perhaps various male climaxes. Youthful women are sufficiently curious to get started with such a guide and look inside. It can fill up as a good friendly exchange to direct the conversing with "any" design you need. The living room is the greatest area to kiss and make out. You can stimulate her with foreplay with your living room chair and lead her with space. Have your condoms close to the bed, which means you will not have to search for an entire lot for them. Make sure they are not in an obvious spot; she can freak out in case she perceives them before you've had sex just for the very first time.

3. The automobile: I do not suggest this spot for having sex with a female just for the very first time. If you elect to undertake it there, make certain you have a little expertise. If you have never had sex in an automobile, it is not the very best idea to get it done using a "stranger." For one point, it is not cozy. I'd an excellent friend was in an automobile with probably the hottest female he would meet, and he couldn't get up through the anxiety. Such things occur... So do not push it, unless you realize she's a sexual and adventurous female, who may be switched on by having sex in the automobile. If the female appears to be much less experienced or perhaps not even prepared for sex, stay away from making use of the automobile.

Allow me to share a couple of things to get when a female is coming:

1. Candles as well as incense: You can purchase specific scented candles. These're helpful resources for establishing the mood. Girls are romantic wildlife, and also they'd prefer to consume by candlelight than by the glow associated with a big, harsh lamp. Yet another sensible plan is a dimmer switch, that you can apply to manage the intensity of your respective burning.

2. Interesting books: a guide about sex, for instance. You can have her remain in the dining area, while you visit the bathroom for a couple of minutes. In case you allow such a guide on the dinner table, it is going to get the attention of her for sure and also provide you with anything to talk about. ☺

3. Exotic or attractive objects: for example, material out of your latest travels in Europe or maybe even in a close-by city. Because many females are wondering, she is going to ask about it, and also you can inform the stories of yours and also have a thing to discuss for some time.

4. Total home and stereo video system: It does not need to be the most beneficial one out there, though you may wish to pay attention to a Cd or even view a hot DVD you rent together.

5. A stack of sound CDs to establish the mood: Applying several kinds of music when she arrives or perhaps while you remain collectively on the couch can help her to calm down. I advocate light or chill-out/ambient rock music because nearly all females that way. Naturally, whatever you participate in, it must reflect The musical taste of yours! Do not enjoy music that is electronic in case you are into the rock only since I recommended it.

The preceding are good examples of common music which must be great for establishing the mood for the date of yours.

6. Liquor as well as ice cubes within the refrigerator: Champagne is likely the very best, nonetheless, even though some basic wine or maybe a few extended drinks as Bailey's is OK. You can likewise find a few good blended drink blueprints on the web and mix mixed drinks for each individual to appreciate, like a climax blended beverage, for instance.

7. Chocolate, whipped lotion, and strawberries great for sex play.

8. Such stuff and bath bombs in the bathroom in case you choose to shower and bathe together.

9. Condoms: obviously. Do not place them in a noticeable spot, but ask them to prepared next to the bed of yours in the drawer. You can additionally purchase stylish sleeves or maybe situations for the condoms of yours.

10. By the manner, I recommend getting a substantial double bed with many major, very soft, fluffy pillows. Women like those.

SEX

As with establishing a date, you will find no secret formulas: whether we are to have sex with a female will count much more on what our interaction with her was like while having to know one another compared to on what moves we make getting to an area where we could be by ourselves, whether that's in a hotel or even again at our place. If there's one thing I am sure of, it's that getting your place significantly enhances the chances of years of sleeping with every female. Inviting her back to your site without implying you're likely to have sex while taking her to a resort might make matters slightly more complicated. Men that exist by themselves, in common, project energy that is different and also displays various behaviors. A male being capable and independent of looking after himself shows having sound survival skills. Whether we have a place of ours or perhaps is not eventually a deciding factor. Her counting on us, on diverse hand, is also the most effective way to get her to believe in us is if it is truthful. Several males are effective with females and state that females need to be lied to which in case you're frank with them you're a "loser".

Provided you can generate a female's trust by being truthful, showing vulnerability, moreover not remaining need, you will have no difficulty sleeping with her, she possibly must undertake it. It might occur over the very first day or even later on which will rely on the experiences you discuss whenever you see. She may have a few reservations or perhaps enforce some kind of friction, such as a non-sex-on-the-first-date rule. Or maybe it may be her first time. Some men are relatively successful with women and say that women have to be lied to and that if you are honest with them you are a "loser". Provided that you can earn a woman's trust by being honest, showing vulnerability, and not being needy, you will have no problem sleeping with her, she will most probably want to do it. It may happen on the first date or later that will depend on the experiences you share when you meet. She might have some reservations or impose some fiction, like a non-sex-on-the-first-date rule. Or it might be her first time.

Remember that it is fundamental to know how to express our sexual desire and do a smooth kino escalation. Imagine we have already kissed her: what can we do to get somewhere more private with her? Mystery Method suggests that one could make an excuse so that the girl will say yes to going somewhere private without feeling like there's too much at stake. For instance:

• I have some amazing colored fish at home, come to see them!

• I'm hungry, let's grab some breakfast!

• I'll show you those photo albums we were talking about, let's go!

But apart from this difficulty, I believe these kinds of excuses are unnecessary when dealing with

Most women nowadays. Seriously, if a girl is interested, she won't need any excuses. If I see things getting hot, I just put it straight to her: "Let's get out of here." or "We can't do this here, why don't we go somewhere else?" Whether or not she accepts will depend on how much she trusts us.

When we have sex with a woman, we are in one of our most vulnerable moments. We are literally in the nude with someone. After sex, there is a notorious increase in the woman's investment in the man and a decrease in his investment in her. This is something that happens almost naturally. Most times, it doesn't happen; she ends up losing interest.

CONCLUSION

Regarding seduction, the ironic factor is, the more attractive and strong a female's presence has on you... the easier it's seducing her when you let yourself believe it and convey it. What I've discovered is not to push a sexy state upon a female that just has an average impact on you. Precisely, why might you waste your time on a person who does not inspire you straight away? Question yourself. Sincerely, do you feel unworthy? Could this be the reason you speak with females who have an average impact on your state? Do you open yourself as average? Here, that must be dealt with. The higher the love we have for ourselves, the higher love we can give to others. Never forget, seduction is a two-way street, it's disgusting. You can't seduce on your own, there have to be two polarizing forces dancing within sexual tension. It's a dance, which you share. If you make it concerning her, she will make it about you and there the hookup is done. But as a male function as the trigger, the rock which stimulates the reaction of her to joining this dance! They often complete this often with a sexual glance, a look, or perhaps a strong present breath... know your role.

How To Flirt With Women

Christian Dane

INTRODUCTION

We all have the power of attraction - the ability to attract people and keep them enslaved. Few, however, are aware of this potential interior, and we imagine attractiveness as an almost mystical trait with the few chosen ones are born and the rest of mortals never will command. However, to realize our potential it is enough understanding what exists in the personality of a person who excites naturally others and develop those same characteristics latent within us. Successful seductions rarely start with an obvious manoeuvre or strategic device. This certainly creates suspicion.

Seductions well start with your personality, your ability to radiate a feature that attracts people and moves their emotions in a way they can't control. Mesmerized by your personality seductive, the victims will not realize their subsequent manipulations. Then, it will be very easy to leave them disoriented and seduced. Seduction is the use of romance or persuasion with the intent to lure another into sex. With that said, this seduction guide is intended for the seducer with the target of seduction in mind. When referring to the target of seduction, a feminine pronoun (her, she, etc.) will most often be used. The first chapter prepares you to seduce, while The second chapter focuses on things you should strictly avoid such as harassment, stalking, and bullying while giving examples to answer questions such as, "When does bullying or harassment cross the line into stalking?" Information following these terms advises about chance encounters alongside approaching a specific person. Tips suggest locations, proper timing, and delve into what she may be thinking. Levels of interest are examined and explanations are offered on how to determine intent. By using well-rounded communication tactics, pertinent choices such as when to proceed or back away are explored. Scenarios are provided to answer 'what-if' questions as well. Subsequent chapters explore topics ranging from pre-date contact through how to set and keep the mood for purposes of a positive outcome. To discuss seduction; various definitions, myths, and facts along with advice regarding individual intentions, interest, and responsibility are shared. In addition to factors such as opportunities and responsiveness, appropriate levels of communication are examined.

PREPARE TO SEDUCE

In this chapter, we are talking about preparing for a good seduction. As we all know, to be successful you have to be prepare because even if the improvisation works sometimes it is not the case when it comes to seducing women. As a beginner, you need a good preparation before getting started.

Seduction has 2 types of arrangements:

1. Psychological or moral preparation

2. Physical preparation

Moral or psychological Preparation: Because you read through this brief article I am going to reveal to you have put forth a tiny trial in honest readiness thinking about the simple fact that I'm some you are resolved to motivate the individual you have all of the time needed and maybe all of the young females within the town of yours. Hence, most particularly, these products are assured to achieve success. With it, you are going to have everything that you'd like in daily life on the entire and in seduction particularly. You surely several preconceived ideas about seduction, women and relationships general, who is blocking you. These are often thoughts such as: believing that it is wrong to seduce, that seduction is manipulation, that sex is bad, that women are difficult, complicated, that you don't deserve to have beautiful women in your life. These thoughts often turn into beliefs, and these beliefs become concrete realities in your life. The ones you are thinking of becoming your reality. Whether it's good or bad for you, whether it's positive or negative, that's how it is. Even if you don't believe in it, or you don't understand why this is how it is, accept it. Then you will have to ask yourself the right questions to know what is important to you. Particularly as regards concerns women. Stop asking yourself the wrong questions or lie to yourself. Tell yourself that you need one or more women in your life. If you are a normal man, with a working penis five out of five, you must have sex in your life without to depend. We have been genetically programmed to meet our needs sexual.

So accept that, no matter what others think, it's a need natural. No longer be ashamed of wanting a woman. Also, accept this right for all the other men on this planet. Do not be jealous, and don't get mad at anyone because he has a girlfriend. Identify all the bad ideas about women, sex, relationships, write them down and replace them with what is beneficial for you and others. For instance, in case you believe it is terrible for others to get 2 to 3 wives, so place yourself in the place of theirs. If it had been you? Were you likely to tell you exactly the same thing? If you are the male of females, would you say it is abnormal? As well as in case it was, feel Do you believe females are unaware of what they're performing? Additionally, females outnumber males by much on this world, and if everybody concentrates on a single, what'll be of the others? At any rate, it's up to help you to develop your own personal opinion there above with most rationalism, without considering the viewpoint of others.

Physical Preparation: We will talk about two things essential to seducing well.

1. **Fitness:** Lazy people know that girls love them guys in great shape who can protect them in case of danger or who have at least enough energy to feel alive and comfortable. If you are fat, or thin and weak, know that you can easily change that with a little sport and good food. So move, move your butt and don't tell me it's difficult because I know it. There is nothing that is achieved by doing nothing. You don't do it for them, do it for yourself first. Know that a little sport will only make you happy as soon as you get used to it. Do whatever sport you like: dance race football

swims as you wish.

2. **The look:** The next thing I would like to inform you about physical planning is the way of yours of dressing. Some individuals exaggerate way too much on this particular subject and stuff the skull of yours with information on what and how you can dress. Men, below are only the fundamentals, the greatest look may be the one that suits you and also you alone. This's neither the appearance of Brad pit

neither which of David Beckham. Me personally, if the clothes admire the requirements below, I bring them:

• Fashionable

• New (more or less)

• Neither too tight nor too wide

• Little or no different colours

• You choose the brand

As for shoes, I prefer shoes but choose depending on your clothes. Do not hesitate to ask around you. Add a bracelet, a watch if you want. Wash, shave, remove the bothering hairs, the nails too, and, I assure you that you are ready to go out and flirt.

HOW TO APPROACH A WOMAN?

In this particular section, we are going to discuss how you can go toward a person since it's among the majority posed inquiries worldwide of seduction. One thing I was frequently concerned about when I started of despondency It was a virtually unimaginable essential me. And I understand that this's the situation for a lot of novices, and actually advanced. We prefer to face the Chinese army of more than two million men than to go and approach even the ugliest woman in the world. Know how to speak, have fun and not take the lead The seducer is expansive. But he doesn't say anything, no matter how. He is direct, sometimes ironic. He is very funny. We get it, or not. We like it or not. He speaks easily to everyone. He is laid, he looks mature when we perceive a tip of the sassy kid he was. He is not one to show his feelings. He keeps his troubles to himself. He looks always calm, casual, but not unstable. It is this apparent certainty that attracts women.

Communication

Communication is without a doubt the best invention of man without the I couldn't be writing this manual since it was created to express ideas, feelings, information among others. Within communication, there are several aspects which are the hearing, sight, smile. Every day we see how people use very ugly communication that lowers self-esteem and makes the environment where we live. Improve that way of addressing the people and more when you talk to a girl. If your first impression is in an aggressive tone you will think you are a clown and pathetic man. But if instead, you approach with a hello or anything else you can think of that is of your wits mind you will like it and with a smile on your lips that show what open you are, how nice and good-natured. A smile implies that you are a person with many friends, easy to please anyone with whom you interact. Further remember to ask questions so that your recipient is at I like you, generating a formidable empathy between them. Look her in the eye to show that you lend her a lot pay attention to everything he says or expresses.

WHAT TO STRICTLY AVOID

Harassment

Any actions that continually pressure or distress someone are classified as harassment. Affectionate displays alongside cleverness are normally great characteristics when properly applied. Unwanted usage of such actions at the introductory phase of a relationship indicates the intent behind the cunning or affectionate attitude is harassment; therefore, any signals from her should be carefully considered. Reluctance, irritability, or unresponsiveness indicates your treatment toward her is harassment. Some may show appreciation for your astute phrasing but, if she shows annoyance (or ignores you), she wants space. Asking about her private life or dropping hints about yours will bring more irritation. Pushing for more information about her is creepy. Insisting that she listens to your hints shows her that you're controlling and selfish. Humorous or clever apologies (if this attitude continues) will solidify that opinion. If you send jokes or seek contact through social networking to someone that does not want the attention, your behaviour also transforms into harassment. If continued, law enforcement and charges may be encouraged. Workplace harassment involves career choices. Organizations do not hesitate to document and file charges which impact your future. A wise decision in this circumstance would be to avoid further contact. This isn't to suggest that you should change your character. It would be savvy to mitigate it and let her become acquainted with you first. Patience and self-reflection are highly encouraged when pondering seduction. Someone may appear willing but you do not know her. She may be naturally flirtatious or affectionate. If that's the case, your patience is not only encouraged.it is required. Because most men are physically stronger than women, you have the upper hand. If your personality overwhelms along with your physique, she feels even more defenceless. If you launch into exploring that vulnerability, you're pressuring her into something in which she is not mentally or emotionally prepared. This must happen first (regarding most women) before she can physically show appreciation. Her vulnerability impacts her mentally, emotionally, and physically. You should not emotionally or mentally manipulate her actions (in your mind) to suit your needs. For example; if she allows you to escort her to a vehicle, her intention is not to be assumed as encouragement. The intent of her could be bringing peace of brain (innocent) or even to be familiar with you should (provocative) though it should stay hers alone. Let her move forward. If she trusts you sufficient to request this, the next move of yours must show regard for that trust. On an equivalent note, darkened places should be stayed away from. Obviously, the path to the car of her could be black that could be a powerful signal of the level of her of vulnerability and demonstrate trust in you. Closer attention to details like this will benefit all over the seduction. If she shows a feeling of vulnerability, brightly lit areas or public places are the wisest choices. Knowing a high level of a vulnerability is present and prompting fear by approaching in darkness implies to her that you cannot be trusted. This is termed implied harassment.

Working inside her space or home (interior custom, plumber, carpenter, etc.) provides you with a lot really a strong position; hence, having a bigger effect on her. Make sure you stay away from individual and just use her with polite conversation plus company is important. There'll be various other places and times to carry by way of a seduction. Some females respond to such sneaky techniques of approach within the space of theirs with dull rejection while others brush it all. Because you do not understand the group where she falls, allow her to direct the manner. A warning...her vague appeal to you might appear amplified in the own home of her but don't hurry making any additional move onto the turf of her. Once again, it is the space of her so allow the freedom of her to use.

Bullying

Bullying is the practice of using power (recognized or not) to gain control of what you desire. An example is forcing someone into an enclosed space so their attention remains on you. Such behaviour as sneaking phone numbers into cell phones is also considered bullying. Any action that steps outside her knowledge is intrusive and indicates bullying. Most often, a response is required and the person being bullied feels violated. Law enforcement routinely becomes involved in this type of unacceptable behaviour. Although many tactics may not appear bullying, if the implied intent is to make you happy regardless of her negative reaction...it is classified as such. Pressure is bullying as well as should not be utilized. Press concentrates on bullying between kids vying for interest though people are equally as responsible for that therapy among relatives and friends. Self-assessment or even treatment is usually recommended whether the patterns come out.

Stalking

Stalking is the compulsive actions engaged in when yearning for control of something or someone. Most often, the compulsive person is aware of their behaviour. Social networking and various tools are sometimes used to aggressively demand attention after being told to stop. Bullying and harassment turn into stalking when one shows up announced or leaves messages repeatedly. even if she previously invites you to a location or to call her, the minute she says, "Stop" means just that from the moment she speaks it. All contact (and attempts) must end. You should close all unwelcome communication including association through digital formats (e-mail, instant messaging, gifts, and snail-mail). If continued, the situation could damage relationships involving friends and family (sometimes involving property). Classification as a stalker is not something easily shed. Various formats make it easier to secretly access and follow others socially.   Aggressively targeting specific individuals who have asked you to stop is illegal. Self-evaluation and exploration through therapy are highly recommended. reluctant, don't rush or think that she's willing to take it further. This may cause her to end it right then. You are also prone to becoming a victim if she develops obsessive behaviour. Female stalkers (although less in numbers than male stalkers) can be particularly vicious. You must be alert to dangerous behavioural patterns from her, too. It may be thrilling to think about the willingness of an obsessed woman but the reality can be truly lethal. A female can inflict twisted forms of disaster when completely rejected. To avoid such cases, minimize heavy flirting and search for healthy associations with women that think similarly. Countless females on the planet would welcome your interest without the use of obsessive patterns or control tactics. If you find yourself involved with an obsessive or controlling female or you are tempted toward that behaviour with one, please seek therapy to explore the surrounding issues.

Complimenting:

It is not difficult to use the incorrect means with words of flattery. Opposite in this article, not to mention there's good, but stay away from exaggerating them. They become weary rapidly. The way you praise her is important a lot: "Oh, you appear very beautiful!" This is lame. You're placing her on a pedestal. You praise her appears she's read this on 1000 occasions now. The looks of her are genes. She cannot affect that here. One more defective one: "Nice ass!" Macho style opposite. This is once again a dumb method to get it done. Praise your buddy 's female for your pal that way, however, not the female you are discovering. In case she is sexy, she would like to become complimented due to her personality, design or maybe common perspective. Nobody does that. She will be flattered by your seeing it. Inform her she's an attractive grin and also you love it when she teeth. Inform her she has good earrings and you love the taste of her. Inform her you love her perfume as well as it has 1 of the favourites of yours. Words of flattery should constantly be limited, with the stage and also simple. "Your eyes look like a 100 glowing stars within the twilight." Leave the business owner with the freelance writers. Just state: "Your eyes are excellent. I love going for a gander at them." The way you converse is considerable. Be noiseless, free and never too much revived while commending her. Discuss steadily, checking out her grin and eyes. Appeal to her like a real Man. Express praise in a reasonable, treating, appealing speech. Be steadily sure regarding the role of yours.

Going physical:

Not coming in contact with her or maybe initiating kissing or even sex is a huge issue. It's the male that constantly needs to come up with the very first action. The female is going to give symptoms which she's ready; you've to flip through them as well as advance appropriately. Should you induce living tangible too soon, she is going to freak away as well as try to escape. When you get it done way too late, she is going to think you are reluctant. It is likewise essential to construct the groundwork. She will not be comfy kissing you in case you have never ever touched her prior to. Touch her from time to time on the arms, hands or shoulders inside an informal manner. It is a regular move to make. There is simply no requirement to head to another intense as well as be a touchy-feely fellow however. Plus, do not overlook, you generally need to function as the camera initiating; she will not get it done for you personally. If you realize she is prepared, go in towards the kiss etc.

Lack of sense of humour

knowing how to distinguish between being "serious" and "bitter", we are attracted to a serious man, who gives himself his place, who does not smile with everyone, but who has charisma, that mix between calm, charismatic and seriously seduces us like crazy.

Roses and presents:

Roses as well as presents are amazing tools in keeping a connection as well as demonstrating a person that she's very vital to you, but not for seducing her. It is a normal misguided judgment you are going to lay her by obtaining her endowments or roses. A man will reward her with which. But precisely why must she be compensated whenever you do not have any idea her? If you venture out with a female, she's often an order for you. Will you purchase blossoms for strangers? No. Will you send out presents to strangers? No. It is fine to do this when you are in line with her, and also she is within love with you She simply laughs at these lame tries. Try separating yourself in the group. Be various. A male does not have to remain within collection. He understands what he desires, as well as he understands the way to obtain it.

Lack of life purpose

women notice when men do not have a clear goal in their life, sometimes it may be that they can have money, but when they do not show creativity, they still do not project more on us, the magic breaks, that can be born. Smart women are aware that money comes and goes and that it captivates us is an entrepreneurial spirit.

Being too sexual, from the beginning of the first dates

Becoming too evident, talking about all their conquests in the way they like to have sex, is that this does not go with an intelligent woman because nobody wants to be a prey, but he wants to be a hunter, the intelligent man understands that everything has its time, you cannot run without knowing how to walk.

THE QUALITIES OF A GOOD SEDUCER

Leadership:

Leadership involves using finding yourself to influence all the frames. It's a stylish characteristic, though it's not regarding interesting others to perform stuff. Guides bring in concert a shared perspective on a collective task. The general characteristics of a leader are self-confidence, resolve, strong imaginative capacity, tolerance, respect towards other people's ideas, and humility to acknowledge mistakes. A great college professor of mine once told me that leadership involves three vital elements: setting an example, setting an example, and setting an example. Yes, setting an example is very important. And there are some other elements which characterize a good leader: they are always trying to find new alternatives, they don't have a reactive attitude towards the world around them, but rather seek to change their surroundings for the better. They can bond with different kinds of people regardless of ideological differences. They dare to leave behind the ways that worked for them in the past and, if necessary, make changes to face the future.

During the process of seduction, acting as a leader may mean to request a woman to carry out a certain task. Flirting by acting as a leader has a stronger effect than using jokes. Taking the lead is a way to show vulnerability, since she may decide to decline the proposal that was made to her. There are many things we can do that are indicative of leadership: asking her out or inviting her to our place, asking her to take us by the hand or the arm, inviting her to take up some activity with us (or to play a game), showing sexual interest, asking her questions about herself, or making some sort of physical contact. Leadership has to do with taking the lead and guiding her where we want to go. Role-playing is a good way of combining the use of jokes with leadership. The idea is to turn the interaction into a game. It must be us who have the position of "authority" in this game.

A good seducer must have good Standards:

Don Juan is definitely known as among the most brilliant seducers on the planet (regardless of his to be a fictional character). A difference is pronounced between Don Juan as well as Giacomo Casanova, because, though, Don Juan is thought to get slept with over 1000 females, Casanova is regarded as a much better seducer, even when, based on the information he stored, his conquests only rose to 122. Precisely why could this be and so? Don Juan slept with additional females, and though he did not have an impressive deal of proper care around the sort of females he conquered, he required any to arrive his way, while Casanova select all those he discovered to be very appealing. But exactly why could this be critical? Aren't many females meant to be equally as useful? Effectively indeed and absolutely not. They're identical within the feeling which they're people. Hotaste's terminology of our tastes, they're not. Should we rest with each and every female that provides us the possibility (regardless of whether we love her or not), next we're almost certainly acting out of desperation and neediness. By this, I do not mean to suggest that we ought to simply be with supermodels or maybe video stars, I mean, that we ought to aim at females that will be torture liking, not our buddy's or maybe our parent 's, but ours. We may be similar to females that are plump, or whatever, hairy, large-breasted, big-nosed, black, brunette, skinny, along with that is absolutely alright. What's crucial is we love them, they meet to what we are going to refer to as our standards. All of us have, once or maybe an additional, buy associated with a female which we did not obtain appealing or perhaps we did not such as a lot permits him among us that has not toss the very first stone. As I've announced before, attractiveness is distant relative, and we're trained by context. Precisely the same female might be thought of differently based on the context we're within. Once this occurs, nonetheless, allow it to function as the difference, not the principle. A male with lower requirements is unappealing. Precisely why would a female wish to be with a male that would not care about changing her with any kind of additional, without discrimination at all? Requirements aren't merely associated with appearance but character. I've travelled from females with that I might have had sex just for a single reason: I did not prefer the manner they acted at a particular time. The issue I am attempting to generate here's it's essential to appreciate ourselves. I am not thinking it's the correct method to cope with the circumstances, since I may also have believed, "I is able to install with what she claims, I just wish her towards the evening, anyway. "Undoubtedly, a few years back I'd have acknowledged even worse phrases. But self-respect makes lots of appeals. It calls for putting as well as setting up borders. Lots of females arrived to me with another frame of mind, and lots of others did not - that is precisely how it was.

Most males use females imagining it's females that perform the picking and also picking which males need to successfully pass the tests of theirs being with them for sales which females happen to be in the place to become selective. "Do you've a boyfriend?", "What's the name of yours?", "Can I purchase you a drink? "They display behavior which provides the thought that females tend to be more critical compared to males (a frame whereby they're given additional importance as compared to what we are), but do we realize them? Can they merit that job? in case we've recognized the female for many years, perhaps she does, but when it's a female we've only achieved, my guess is in case she does not. The sort of females we're with says there is a great deal regarding just who we're. It's the same for our choice of pals. As a result, in case we're unhappy with the buddies we've or maybe we do not similar to the females we're with, at this time there are most likely a lot of points regarding ourselves that we're unhappy with. This does not imply we are going to discriminate or even mistreat anybody we do not especially love, though we will not encounter exactly the same affinity with every person. If perhaps we've a far pickier, much less needy style, plus healthy foods worth ourselves and also the individuals we decide to discuss our life with, in that case our behavior is going to be a lot more appealing.

Dress properly

If you wish to be seen by a female, appear appropriately. Focus on dressing correctly in case you believe you can meet up with a person you prefer inside a bar, in a get-together, or maybe a unique occasion. Choose gorgeous, flattering clothing. If you're concerned that the current wardrobe is too dismal, attend a mall. You can consult a saleswoman in case she can assist you in a complementary outfit. Remember: staying yourself is attractive. Attempt to look just like you can on your own terms. This comprises no shave whether you enjoy using a beard, or perhaps not using a fit in case you're of a slightly more informal sort. You won't be comfy in case you're not yourself. This is something your date will notice instantly, and confidence being the primary key to seduction. Have a bath prior to going away and perhaps make use of just a little eau de toilette. An excessive amount can penetrate, but a bit of splash associated with a traditional scent could assist you.

Perfuming for seduction

Most of us secrete odorous chemical things that take part in an important component of precisely how we are considered by others. The latter, that activates replies between people today of the same species, pursues a crucial task within the birth and also upkeep of are after. The fragrance is in the middle of our mental associations besides our relationship with others: doesn't the interpersonal bulk prefer us to use perfumes to hide the body smells of ours? The evocative power of perfume is useful. The perfume that we seduce could possibly be the principal thing we use flawlessly, the individual with which we are it. The fragrance that changes heads since it suits us the same as a glove might be the individual that sublimates our pure scent. The perfume next just envelops the entire body, having a sensual aura. We do not conceal operating the scent of it: we think it! We, for that reason, choose a fragrance with that we think is at great ease since it embodies the image we would like to exhibit. Avoid spraying far too generously, throughout the risk of changing "casserole". We discover the art and the way of perfuming wonderfully by concentrating on the pulsation reasons behind the body: neckline, the inside on the wrist, hollow of the elbow, during the back on the ear.

Seduction starts off with the art form type of perfuming the entire body. The perfume was not supposed for getting just dabbed and applying it would to get absorbed directly to your skin and also mingle together with your sweat to boost your body's fragrance. Throughout the functioning working day, since you sweat, the sweat will distil through the amount of scent and also morph right into a new fragrance that has been extraordinary for you. the strategy you, the fragrance of yours, and additionally it definitely was the smell that had to get lodged to the consciousness of the enthusiast of yours and is reminiscent of all the tips you would market jointly, these kinds of that whenever you made like, the fragrance of yours would blend higher your lover's every and each sensing with recollections of earlier delights besides the delights arrival of concern. Each element of the entire body had to be perfumed with a unique fragrance. every scent was exclusive, though merged in the same way as a transforming though composite whole; you may notice perfumes apart, but it's been hard to discover a way where an individual has also done it; another individual started off. It definitely would have been a seashore of intoxicated sensory faculties with no collection staying for lucid notions.

Seduction was not an event, it definitely would have been a disposition, a feeling, a drive that originated out of the soul and also demanded a while to create higher. Perfume's lured mental faculties, along with the lethargic, languorous movements of brilliantly scented oils becoming rubbed straight into the complete body, will offer a female a far more advanced exhibit of arousal and prepare her for each evening of lovemaking. Likewise, men and women wore perfume, the perfuming rituals of women needed for an extended moment and also when which was a lot more complicated. For women, perfuming was completed immediately after the tub likewise may consume a selection of deals for several hours. Their arms had been the biggest uncovered portion of their entire bodies, so they had been perfumed as beautified. The perfuming of the underarms was a lot more complex. Based on the Kama Sutra, the armpit is an essential erogenous zone. There's a sizable erotic nerve which specifically links the underarm with all the vulva and kissing the armpit induces the females like fluids. The perfume would have been a better way of living. Garments, bedrooms, bathwater were all perfumed. The Kama Sutra advises enthusiasts to always keep the distilled fragrances of citrus and cardamom by the foundation at nighttime in deep situation the beloved fouled upwards the environment by passing blowing wind! There seems to be absolutely no spot for terrible odours on the planet of seduction. Males have been rubbed vigorously with various perfumed oils right before their bath, a workout which probably takes as much as 2 a long time it wasn't almost scenting the entire body but additionally producing the proper disposal which will be arousing for the partner of his. As soon as the footbath, an infinitesimal amount of additional fragrance was reapplied to certain areas of the body vulnerable to far more sweat, the focus staying on 'very little' because males just applied tiny levels of perfume. The quantity of perfume you used was the distinction within the station in life. Guys with reduced breeding used large levels of fragrance that induced them to reek of it. Guys, in addition, used floral garlands of many types, most with their own fragrances, to look into the scent of sweat on their necks and brows. The blossoms had been picked based on the time of year, the time and also the event.

The arms were definitely the largest uncovered component of the entire body to ensure they'd been perfumed too as they were beautified. The perfuming of the underarms was an impressive deal more complicated. In line with the Kama Sutra, the armpit is an extremely important erogenous zone. There is a large erotic nerve that exclusively links the underarm with all of the vulvae along with kissing the armpit brings about the females just like fluids. The perfume will have a far better lifestyle.

Garments, bedrooms and bathwater were each perfumed. The Kama Sutra in fact advises fanatics to constantly maintain the distilled perfumes of cardamom and citrus by the groundwork at nighttime wearing serious circumstance the beloved fouled higher the earth by passing blowing wind! There appeared to be hardly any area for dreadful odours within the earth of seduction. Guys are rubbed vigorously with different perfumed oils directly prior to their water, an exercise session that could take as much as two a very long period. It was not nearly scenting the entire body but in addition, creating the disposition that will arouse for the partner of his. The moment the bath, with a small quantity of extra scent reapplied to particular parts of the body that had been susceptible too much more sweat, the main focus remaining on 'almost no bits' just apart, started using men on a training course using small amounts of perfume. The volume of perfume you used was the difference inside the station in deep lifestyle. Men of decreased breeding used enormous amounts of scent, which induced them to reek of it. Men additionally switched to using floral garlands of countless kinds, most with all their perfumes, to check out the fragrance of sweat on their brows and necks. The blossoms were definitely selected depending on the time of the season, enough time besides furthermore, the event

Taking it slow

Seduction is not with no timing. The outlook is a huge component of exactly why one individual wants yet another. If you come across a female you are keen on, go gradual. Hold out for just a little prior to talking with them andtune in a lot more than you talk. Do not make the intentions of yours apparent instantly, or else you might place them off. Go gradually, a minimum of in the beginning.

Pay attention to the nuances to understand women

In the event that you would like to much better comprehend the dialect of females, you've to focus on the nuances. Males voice the needs of their straightaway. Ladies, however, transmit concealed info which the counterpart of their needs to acknowledge themselves. They offer tips concerning whatever they love, what they're attracted to as well as expectation you are going to take it upwards and also understand it yourself. For males that wish to recognize the psyche of females, this's usually hard to understand, progression as well as fully understand. In the event that you would like to learn the thing that makes females tick, it's thus vital that you pay attention to the signs which she directs you. Just about everything matters. It starts off while you talk towards the female. Does she send back your eye communication if you go over during her? Does she laugh? She blushes and after that appears out? These're many indicators which she's keen on you. In the event that you would like to understand the body words of females, you have to realize these specifics.

Listen

The way you speak with her can make an enormous difference in between becoming rejected, essentially acknowledged solely as a buddy or even awakening unimagined feelings and passions. In the event that you wish to achieve success within the art form of seduction, you have to figure out how to communicate. Once you talk to a female, make an effort to enjoy her. Lots of individuals are attracted to people who demonstrate to curiosity within them. So, rather than bragging in relation to your successes as well as revealing to the own stories of yours, try out listening thoroughly rather. Make an effort asking a lot more concerns as compared to what you answer. Question questions that are simple to kick the ice. Try out, for instance, "How would you create a living?" And "Where did you develop up?" Always serve as in case you're listening very carefully. Laugh, nod, as well as sometimes publish a comment as "Exactly" or "aha". Question follow up issues. Feel free to make clear or even give much more comprehensive information on personal information and a story.

Sexual appeal is clearly associated with character. Obtaining to find out somebody much better may even increase your sexual feelings of yours for that individual. in case you attract the female, you might delight in having more sex with her in case you've greeted her prior to.

Asking the Right Questions to Extract Values

To be in a position to draw out values correctly, you want it to provide the fundamental values of yours and also to accomplish that; you have to perform the proper issues. For instance, you are able to begin with: "I feel the sensation of understanding yet another man getting is wonderful. And also what's revitalizing is learning what another person believes on the subject of the planet around us as well as learning what's essential within existence because of this someone else. Everything you appreciate as well as what is crucial for you inside a relationship? ". When she does respond with ultimate values (feeling adored as well as understood) "ready!" Be the main thing that can make the feel of her that manner When she answers with travelling values, check with one more query, these kinds of for example: "And just how does that help to make you feel? So why do you enjoy it?"

Focus on talking about what emotions she feels and why emotions. Ask questions, listen to her answers and you'll never be without subject to talk to her. You must know who you must be to be with her. How can you get this? It is simpler than you think. Instead of staying talking about your new car or the car you want to buy, ask her about herself and pay attention. It would not be appropriate to just go around asking a lot of questions. That it may seem rehearsed and you can never give that impression. It would be too more natural if you introduce the questions in a friendly conversation.

Example:

"You understand what, I realize that inside a circumstance as this specific, the standard issues to become directed are "what will you do?" and such things as that. in the event that I requested, what part might you locate difficult within that which you do, both since you have to concentrate far too much on it or perhaps since you want additional inspiration, etc., what would that be? " A very important detail is that you should never ask nonsensical questions because it's going to look very strange and you're going to get worse. What you to do is connect one question to the other and thus start a new topic from a derivation of the initial topic.

Her: Me too ... That's why I prefer to have my corner just to

 me ... bla bla bla.

You may have noticed how in the example above the topic changes are all subtle and related. Neither you nor she had to change the topic roughly. Pay attention to the derivation of each topic and you will always have something to say. The wrong and as most unsuccessful way leads a conversation is like this:

You: What is the next step?

She: Bla Bla Bla ...work with children

You: Have you always lived with your parents?

Her: No, they broke up when I was 10.

You: Do you live alone?

She: (she thinks, "because that ta guy doing me this questionnaire")

You must seem genuinely interested in her life. Make questions superficial about her life and then go to more questions important. She will only answer more personal questions to someone she likes, then make the connection with her first, then stays interested in her and she will like the fact that someone wants to know things deeper about it. Rather than just looking interested, you can try to genuinely interest. I just genuinely care about who she is and I feel curious about her too, how she feels, what she thinks and what you believe. But I always keep my goal in mind. If she has beliefs other than yours, do not argue with her or fully agree with it (if you do not agree). There is one way to escape this situation: Ask her to try to convince you. Say something like "I have a different opinion on this. I think you must have a good reason to think that way. I am curious, how did you come to these conclusions? What convinced you? As would you convince anyone of that? What she is sure to give you is the strategy of convincing herself.

IMPORTANT: This information can be excellent to convince you about other matters. She's showing you exactly how it forms its opinion cork matters.

Be self-confident/ self-esteem

Self-confidence, alongside confidence, is an indisputable soil for seduction. They attract the vast majority of people to self-confidence. If you have faith in yourself, it's about to entice extra people. Therefore, attempt to act confidently when achieving a female, you want. In addition, recall the sequence within between self-confidence and also egomania thins away. Once you eliminate a conversation to brag associated with yourself, that's daunting. Although it is perfectly acceptable if you are pleased with yours, the lineage of yours together with some other info on the life of yours is the thing you have requested for. Develop a laugh for her. It attracts plenty of people to people with an excellent sensation of humour. Attempt to take significant advantage of the entire encounter, in addition, to determine if you're competent enough to impress the female with the comedic aspect you have. To have and, above all, develop good self-esteem, it is enough to follow the following principles:

- Be forgiving with yourself when you commit errors.
- Focus on your strengths and successes.
- Learn to say "no".
- Reject indifferent remarks with indifference.
- Consider everyone as your equal.
- Know how to appreciate mistakes and learn from them.
- Make happiness a habit.
- Accept being wrong with serenity.

- Stop railing against yourself.

- Find a job that suits you.

- Don't worry about the image you give.

- Accept yourself unconditionally today.

- You deserve better than you think.

- Recover freedom.

- Give yourself a parenthesis of pleasure every day.

- Be prepared to commit in the desires of yours.

- Ask yourself what makes people tell you that you have them seriously injured.

- Your opinion of yourself must be paramount.

- Be 100% positive one day a week.

- Admit that people are different from you.

- Determine your definition of perfection.

- Resist the urge to change so that others love you.

- Do not compare yourself to anyone. Being different should not disturb you.

- Avoid causing yourself unnecessary pain.

- Stop identifying with your actions.

- Give importance to your wise decisions.

- Prioritize your opinion of yourself.

- Take charge of your health.

- Keep smiling when criticized.

- Know how to adapt.

- Forge your opinion and make your decisions.

- Accept compliments with good grace.

- Give importance to your ideas.

- Learn to do the tasks you assign to yourself other.

- Do not take any kind of competition too seriously.

- Your personal needs are the most important.

- Have a fair view of others.

- Say "no" to guilt.

- Think you are a worthy person.

- Forgive yourself for all your faults.

- Interpret each event positively.

Humour

Humor will be the art form of interaction is essential to consult with someone since it provides values of becoming an enjoyable, helpful individual as well as with a lot of buddies round. The advice of mine: Don't build jokes the objective of mine isn't this particular, but you utilize in the vocabulary of yours a bit of sensory faculties of humor just like misrepresenting small things to become good for you. An excellent instance of this is the to adhere to you wind up chatting mentally using a female on top of an unexpected she says to you: The buddy of mine as well as I showed up in concert 2yrs returned. To you act in response with the following symptom You are among a number of several people I have found which has lasted this specific long partner, exactly how lengthy maybe you've been with her. What if he is sure that he will respond with a beautiful smile on his lips one of those that one loves to receive after action and not repeat many times "What is repeated many times loses quality" When it comes to humor, laugh as little as possible at your jokes, Of course, with this,

I do not tell you to always be serious but to be a type fun to say an alpha seducer.

Calibrating the Woman

When you are able to begin making her feel great, extract and even understand the values of her, mirror them to her, provoke excitement and desire, etc., you've to learn how to understand your certain indicators great, neutral or bad. Naturally, several indicators are evident. If perhaps she's a look enormous naturally she's pleased. Within the exact same manner, like she's crying it's feasible to deduce that she's depressing. Nevertheless, the indicators aren't constantly which distinct. So that you can obtain a lot more details on the way the female responds to every design that you simply comment, every issue you consult or maybe every path you consult you to opt for the chat, you have to adjust the reactions of her. Find out, by asking questions, how she behaves when she agrees with something. Discover the same way it behaves when it doesn't agree and when it is neutral. You can tell her it's a game or you're practising your psychic abilities, asking her to think of something she fully agrees from the bottom of your heart. She doesn't need to tell you that she thought and it's even better that she doesn't say. Then ask her to think of something you feel neutral with. Then ask her to think of something that she strongly disagrees with. Repeat this cycle a few times. Then ask her to think about anything and that you, based on your observation, will guess if she agrees, feels neutral or not agree. Play this game for a while and then stop and move on to another thing. Another way for you to identify her calibration and look closely when she talks about things she adores or fully agrees with. see the way she talks, facial and body expressions. This's way too a great deal important. After a while of conversation, you will have valuable information about how she reacts to each feeling. With that, you can direct the talk in the right direction. Ex: Notice how she is normally and then notice when she mentions (usually with expressions of joy, affection, longing) your pet, a cat or dog. Then you ask "and your cat/dog ever hurt? " After that question "does your puppy wake in place quickly within the morning?" and observe her alter her face once again. It's a wonderful advantage you will have if you recognize easy methods to look at the response to her. You'll normally understand whether the points you're getting into for coming out as the winner it works or perhaps not. For instance, if you turn up much closer to a female, she understands what you are attempting to perform, and she has to be apparent to you the way she thinks regarding it. An optimistic hint can cause a kiss, a bad since it requires you to do the job more difficult on a chat. When you do not identify the signal, you might wind up risking a kiss with an incorrect period and then destroy every insignificant thing.

Address your emotions

After that question "does your puppy wake in place quickly within the morning?" and observe her alter her face once again. It's a wonderful advantage you will have if you recognize easy methods to look at the response to her. You'll normally understand whether the points you're getting into for coming out as the winner it works or perhaps not. For instance, if you turn up much closer to a female, she understands what you are attempting to perform, and she has to be apparent to you the way she thinks regarding it. An optimistic hint can cause a kiss, a bad since it requires you to do the job more difficult on a chat. When you do not identify the signal, you might wind up risking a kiss with an incorrect period and then destroy every insignificant thing.

The key to a successful first date comes from your emotional world. You should always make this clear when it comes to understanding women. You can reach your inner self by focusing on things that are relevant to you. External impressions can trigger emotions. It's less about how you look or status icons. You have to convince them of your personality. Because for men the first incentive to flirt is often determined by sexual attraction, for women it is more important what a man conveys, what he stands for, what defines him.

How do women understand? Make her feel right

Be helpful, courteous, open, and honest. If you would like to find out exactly how females belong as part of like, a signal which you're self-confident but also can display thoughts. Use your humour, report your personal goals, show you have a program for your life. These are all topics that women appreciate. They make sure that your date feels comfortable with you. Because that's exactly what it's all about if you want to understand how women feel and think: moments and memories that they combine with a feeling. After the appointment, she will not remember which car you drove up to. But she'll still know how she felt with you.

Smile

More important than your words are your smile. Smile and do it with grace, without nervousness, showing security. The smile shows happiness, and everyone we like happy people; It is also contagious, so don't wait for her Smile, do it yourself and surely she will smile. By smiling you will send the message that you are fun, you have ease of generating Empathy, and most importantly: she will never be bored with you. A smile shows that you are a person with many friends that gives him a lot of confidence in you since he sees you as a man who can understand people. It makes the conversation more enjoyable remember to give to receive so smile first. Suggests there's sufficient interaction and for individuals are near you say that you're a male of a great sling, show to you're not among those who hold the uphill problems of theirs though they get out of him in your home and also attempt to provide their utmost within the area of seduction, suggest that you receive with those individuals with whom you talk in that second, A look motivates an individual who's within which depressing time, The look means that you don't lifeless; you battle with whatever they let you know and also you create a good example in case they let you know one thing you do not love when you're inside a team also you're feeling uncomfortable do not squander the words of yours on its own you smile along with depart. The one who did this to you, you will leave with great fury for not having realized your dreams which were to displease you. In short, a smile is a health, being a very healthy person spiritually.

Be funny without being a joke

By definition, seduction is a way of expressing our sexuality in a manner that women will find attractive without looking needy, which is always a plus in terms of attraction. The most frequently used seductive techniques are joking around or making fun of the other person. Some people have taken to learning techniques and concepts such as Negs, Cold Readings, Push & Pull, Cocky & Funny. Some others do magic tricks, play rock-paper-scissors or resort to magazine-like tests, or talk about the zodiac signs, and so on. All these techniques share a common purpose: seduction.

But seduction is not everything in itself: you may be the funniest guy of the group or the one with the best magic tricks, but if you don't advance sexually. You will inevitably end up falling into the friend zone. Our ability to seduce is closely linked to our social skills. The better our seductive skills, the better responses we will get from women. Seduction can be carried out by joking around or assuming a leadership role. Both these techniques must be applied with honesty and self-sufficiency. Joking and leadership work because they subliminally communicate little emotional investment from our part. If she responds positively, then she is investing more in us. Now, for instance, if we make a joke about her coat and she gets upset or doesn't try to keep our acquaintance, the chance is she is not interested in us. Precisely the same occurs with leadership: if she doesn't come along when we suggest going somewhere, or she doesn't fulfil our requests, then it is probable she doesn't want anything with us. An example could be that we ask her to come with us to get a drink at the bar or to go to the drugstore, but she prefers staying with her friends.

So far as jokes and also mockeries go, it's essential

to bear in your mind that creating a witty persona is much more critical compared to understanding the funniest jokes. If you don't like someone, you won't find them funny. But humour is a key element in attraction. Women laugh when they are with men to whom they feel attracted, and men, on their part, feel attracted to women who laugh with them.

Several amusing attitudes that can be employed when seducing are listed below:

- Misinterpreting what women say: For instance, if she says "shall we do it" (no matter

the context), we could answer, "Hey, I think you are going too fast. "Exaggerating what she

says or does: We could resort to lines like, "This purse is huge! Are you carrying a gun?", or,

if she were holding a green drink, "That looks radioactive. "If she said something

like "I'm having a bad hair day", we could observe "I did not wish to convey anything at all, but

224

today you bring up it..." (take proper care to not cross the series with regards to issues of age or looks —if she states she says she is body fat, stay away from revealing to her she will look in the videos as a whale). Making funny associations: Try to connect the situation you are in with elements from

popular culture, whether it be TV programs, movies, books, etc.

- Fishing for sexual innuendo: If she says she is cold, we could tell her, "You are not getting a hug from me" If she says she's hot, we could remark, "It's just that you are standing too close to me" If she asks, "How long? "we could say something like, "Shall I get something to measure it?"

Another great way to mock her is to combine a strong criticism (said in a playful tone) with a sincere compliment. For instance, "Those yellow shoes make you look like the cutest clown ever", or, if she cannot make up her mind about something, you could tell her, "So much indecision will get you into trouble, you're too smart for that. "It is a bittersweet combination. It can cause an excellent perception, and also it's not necessarily crucial that criticism, and opposition, is attached. Making use of sarcasm is also quite polarizing, although, for that same reason, it can be quite affronting. This is a kind of ironical humor not meant to be hurtful, and it works in a subliminal rather than on a direct level, but there are moments when it can be out of place. Sarcasm is the hardest kind of humor to communicate via text message. One ought to be careful when doing so. It is important not to be excessive, to not try to force anything to keep the conversation going, it has to be more or less natural. When it comes to humor, jokes always work better if one keeps a straight face, and instead of laughing hard tries to keep it to the bare minimum. Cracking a joke while keeping an impassive look on one's face causes a greater impact. It is also helpful to read books by comedians or watch their videos, and to pay attention to the use of humor-generating techniques mentioned above. It doesn't hurt to look for jokes or amusing lines, but it is not what makes a difference. Within cases that are many, they'll most likely appear furious. And also below we're planning to need to master to make sure whether or not it's since they sensed offended, or even since they're attempting to obtain the attention of ours. It may also happen that she smiles but took offence in what one said. Not all jokes are well received by any girl in any situation. If they overplay their anger, then we are probably on the right track. But if she were upset, then perhaps we went too far. In that case, it is best to simply offer her an apology.

THE POWER OF THE LOOK

The look, as the name well says, has incredible force since This shows consideration you have never heard. "The eyes are the reflection of the spirit" They contain all the enchanting intensity of an individual, they state a great deal from you. They show the moods you have at that moment and thanks to them you can see that girl you like so much. Regarding if looking at a girl is bad, no, it is very good and natural that you do it but always in the eyes never direct your look towards other "parts" unless it is turned from back at that time. You should almost always look her straight in the eye if she looks down shows that she is a shy person, if she keeps it fixed it is a girl temperamental and they are the ones that you will surely love. When you are with her look her in the eye, this is so important that it guarantees the victory. Most people do not look others in the eye but rather direct their look the other way or focus the whole face, this reflects fear and generates in the interlocutor the feeling that they are hiding something from you or lying to you. Because you do not wish to come up with that here sensing inside the female inside front side individuals must appear her within the eye, still in case you haven't but released yourself or perhaps crossed term simply appear her inside the eye as well as hang on for the reaction of her.

The psychological effect of gaze is so powerful that you should not miss it. Also, your reaction It will indicate the type of girl she is: If she looks down, she is shy, if she holds it, it is romantic and temperamental if she holds it and also smiles at you, it is yours. Such a strategy is especially effective since it shows you're thinking about it; you're not searching for what everybody else is searching for (although they search). By doing this, she appreciates you as somebody reliable and can feel cost-free to open up the soul of her. If perhaps she answers the question of yours with no evasion you've become on the subsequent fitness level.

SHYNESS

If you ask me what is shyness in seduction, I answered that it is not having women. I advise you that there is no nothing more beautiful than to be liberally clear always with something of sanity, of course you know what I mean by this. What He tried to explain to you that you are reading to me that this is a problem since it does not allow you to approach that woman that you like so much or not so raw so it leaves a trace of nervousness that the first that she will understand is that you are extremely interested in her and what is sure to manipulate and use you the truth is raw but it's that simple you have to face it with a lot of courage and stand every day in the mirror and tell yourself I'm not shy and face it. How do you deal with this situation when you see a little girl out there sitting alone you approach him with a smile and you start a talk as if you were talking to someone who you know of all the life without pain when speaking or nothing? If you see angry at lake tell her to excuse me or is a joke that will suffice. If at, On the contrary, the shy is your partner, that can be faced with the help from a seducer like you by showing him that fear doesn't should be part of your life but face it all problems that come to you. Making her overcome her fears makes me trust you more and the answer is with sex or other things.

Understand body language

Body language is a fundamental element of seduction since it shows our degree of availability, attraction, interest and sensuality. Some signals are unconscious, making it impossible to control and understand them, but others are deliberate, and it is on these that you must focus. If you can interpret body language and actions from others, you will get more information about their feelings. In this way, you will know who likes you and you can engage relationships easily in your work and social life. When communicating with a person, know that only 7% of what you say is picked up by your interlocutor through the spoken words, and the rest is communicated through your body language. You can then note the austerity and primordial importance of Your Body Language. In general, communication is done through several elements:

- The tone of voice
- Intonation
- Movements and gestures
- Facial expression
- The flow of speech

- The way to walk
- Breathing

At first, we say to ourselves, but why and how to treat it all? Simple answer: The Body language sub-communicates everything you have behind the head. For example, when you are in a room with people, you can easily identify who is nervous, happy, sad, excited etc. Do this exercise next time when you're in a waiting room, and try to guess the state of each person with you in the room Let's connect it all with seduction. Body dialect is an element of the toolbox of females. By, I mean, the "Detection" of Body Language. A female can readily know very well what you're attempting to point out, everything you project by the picture you use your car with the body language of yours. If, for example, you are dressed like a tramp, if you stink of fish and, if you walk like a penguin, hardly hope to seduce a girl with your sales pitch and your blah of three times nothing (And your openers stupid sometimes) A very easy way will help us understand the issue of body language It is noticed by men with a royal Body Language. Look at the big one's actors like Brad Pitt, Tom Cruise or charmer George Clooney, The athletes' high levels like David Beckham with his class and elegance, Politicians and great managers of companies. They all have, and without exception, the perfect body language, you must have!!!! Notice their way of speaking, walking and behaving ... You go fast to understand that they are calm and completely sure of themselves and their attitude, we have the impression that they control the weather. They give off so much confidence amazing that we just want to listen to them and be with them, in other words, and thanks to their just perfect body language, these great world figures we sell happiness!

Now let's go to the practical part and let me show you and point out the signs of bad body language that a man adopts in front of a woman, during a seduction report:

- He speaks very quickly (nervous)
- He talks a lot (story to impress him)

- He stalls and doesn't know what to say after
- He asks TOO * stupid * questions
- He talks waving his hands in all directions, like crazy!
- He looks around while speaking to see if others are looking at him
- (zero confidence !!!)
- When he helps, he appears down
- He is absolutely not grinning
- he is not in the least self-assured! Frankly, men... what might you think about such a guy? Exact! A little geek and a first-class looser, who can NEVER dream of seducing a woman.

Now let's try to fix these details:

- Do not put your hands in the pockets
- Never lower your eyes when you walk... Look to the horizon
- Take big steps while walking
- Take care of your physical appearance and your look, do not dress like a civil servant.
- Walk with CONFIDENCE!

- Touch women when you talk to them non-sexually of course (shoulders, forearms, back, feel their hair ...)
- Don't look away when you're talking to a woman
- Always have a sexy little smile
- When you're in a cafe, don't bend over when she's talking to you lean, Backstep back and let her lean toward you.

The strength of words is important in people doing something some are always hurting internally saying things that not even your worst enemy, this favours your self-esteem to decline and this leads to one thing you stop being independent of yourself same, which I mean by this that all the actions that do for yourself have to be treated first by your friends and how many other people on the list who you ask a lot of advice daily. What you should do from now on is say words that Motivate to continue something for example. I'm going to flirt with this little girl and I'm sure she will be my girlfriend.

The Importance of Empathy

In the game of seduction whoever wins the prize is the most skilful in the art of generating empathy, and one of the easiest ways to generate it is through imitation. Therefore, to achieve magnificent results with it, imitate it, observe what do and do it yourself, without being too obvious: If you cross your arms, cross them, if you touch the hair wait a moment and do the same when he smiles he smiles too. If she is speaking very slowly you must speak very slowly too, yes do it quickly do it the same. Imagine that there is a mirror in between the two, and plays at being his reflection.

Empathy is nothing more than coinciding with the person you are talking is a true art and not only manifests itself in the language but also in body language an example of empathy is next.

Him: -Tell me and what subjects do you like about the classes that you receive.

She: - Spanish

Him: - Or that was also my favourite subject, I don't know

because but I loved it. And tell me why you like it so much?

She: - Nothing just that I like to write, I hope to read one day be a good writer like many world-renowned writers.

Him: - I am certain you'll, ...

As you can see here it is closed in a simple dialogue like boy generates empathy in the communication process.

Try appropriate pick-up sayings

Pick-up or rip-off sayings have a bad reputation. But if you use the right saying - one that is not used too often or greasy - this can emphasize your charm and arouse the interest of the woman. The examination of shows that have dedicated themselves to this topic shows that highlighting good qualities - that is, a little bit of showing off -

can be helpful. Women react less to pick-up lines that only contain empty compliments or are sexual. They seem to respond more to pick-up lines where they learn about the strange man that makes him stand out from the crowd. If you are a nurse, for example, you can try something like: "Phew, pretty lifeless party, what? As a nurse, I would have declared the patient dead a long time ago. "Or, in case you are a firefighter, you can attempt this:" Could it be me or could it be boiling only in with these? As a firefighter and a high-temperature pro, I am determined for you to be a source. " Should you select an expression, think about something brilliant that spotlights an issue of your personality or maybe your life? Attempt to do your job in case it's intriguing, or maybe several of your hobbies, or perhaps optimistic characteristics. But don't just escape it at which. Studies show that makeup sayings do the job better when and then a chat.

Provide security and give each other space

If you want to understand women, it should

be clear to you that a relationship is also about feeling good together. You can accomplish this through several things. It is typically a woman to look for traditional values such as security, trust, respect, someone to lean on, a partner with equal rights in a relationship. You want to feel comfortable with the man at your side.

Important: At the same time, things like personal freedom become more important. You should keep that in mind if you want to understand how women think. These days, they no longer just work in the relationship, they need time for themselves, they want to develop further. To guarantee this particular, it's vital, honestly, to give consideration to info as well as to be for continual dialogue.

Chance Meetings and Opportunities

Let's say you haven't spoken to her but know her name and you run into her by chance in public. A simple, "Hello (say her name), what a pleasant surprise…" is a great way to begin. At this point, anxiety is completely normal. The meeting was unplanned so you'll need to think fast. Something to consider: you should not attempt physical greetings such as a handshake, hug, kiss on the cheek, etc. (unless she initiates it). There are various reasons. She may need a buffer of space, suffer from an allergy to manufactured scents, or have embarrassingly sweaty palms. Try for some kind of ice-breaker while paying close attention to her body language but concentrate on your words. Since you need her positive response; factors such as location, time, and her attitude should be carefully considered. When she does reply, be prepared if the conversation veers off in another direction. Your alertness to surroundings will benefit you greatly. Attempt something unique (yet appropriate). If observant to certain factors (location, dress, and timing), the information you gather from her body language, dress, and tone can be used to tailor your response. For example; if you stumble across her after both of you have an emergency maintenance issue with lawn care equipment, ask for details. Don't give advice but do give a glimpse of your similar emergency. The two situations can be playfully compared with joint pondering and contemplation following. It sets the tone for the relationship, creating a memorable condition in which to bring up in the future. even if there are only one or two dates, this impression shows her a genuine person with whom she can relate.

What Else Do I Say?

You will find unusual instances exactly where commenting on the appearance of her is appropriate. In case she understands that you are a physician, you might flirt within this specific manner. Or else stay away from that individual region. You will probably imagine, "Why not note that she is attractive?" Many people encounter various amounts of self-analysis out of 1 day to another. You have absolutely no way of recognizing in case this's 1 of the better days of her. If she is today creating a terrible working day, your remarks might inadvertently sour her mood and further earn potential exposure to her discomfort. Also, she may think that's the only reason for your approach. If she believes her appearance is your only attraction, she won't relax around or take you seriously. We all know that appearance is important when trying to win someone over. Besides, we all have life's little emergencies where we need to rush out during plumbing or yard work for much-needed supply. If this happens, be aware of what you're wearing. That grass-stained, grease-streaked shirt and ripped jeans may be perfect for working on your mower but might now work too well if she's on her lunch break from her office job. If you see her, it would be best to tactfully nod as greeting (you don't want to be rude and ignore her). However, if she's sporting the same emergency vibe and type of wear, you just landed an opportunity to connect.

The day and the time have come for you to call her,

the following are basic points to keep in mind before raising the horn and marking:

• The phone call must be brief; you cannot capture too much time we talk about things which it's far better to mention it individually.

• She can only listen to you, so you should try to speak clearly and not demonstrate any kind of nervousness that is reflected in a trembling voice and sometimes nasal, stuttering or prolonged silence.

• Write down the most important thing you want to try to avoid prolonged silence and nervousness.

• Remember some important aspect that she has told you and ask the respect to show that you care about her and paid attention to her.

• Agree on the date, time and place of your next personal meeting.

• Begin by greeting her after which check with her in case she is not overly hectic or maybe you interrupt her for one thing, you'll teach admire for the time of her as well as in exactly the same period, you are going to make certain they provide you with the full attention of theirs.

• Before saying goodbye, tell her to say hello to her family, if she meets them at that time.

THE PLANNED MEETING

Conference regions are important and also must be proper. You will find many locations to meet a certain somebody (or maybe female). Stay away from the conference in a bar, nightclub, or maybe dance club in case you are looking for a long-lasting connection or maybe one thing with the material. Until you're finally able to understand her much better, the region produces a lot of diverse indicators that result in confusion. There are many places to meet, however, a good deal of might need a lot more preparation. For instance, going to a program at her church might seem ideal. First, consider the social atmosphere in which you will manoeuvre. If selected, plan to arrive early and stay late to avoid speaking during the sermon. She may be very attentive and classify distractions as rude behaviour. As a side note, avoid attending a specific denomination unless you have plans to join such. You may give her the wrong impression. If a particular church does not reflect your genuine self, it is unwise to mislead her into thinking that it does.

Another consideration is with whom did she attend? If she has children with her, they will occupy any excess time and attention. If you see her shopping at a department or grocery store with children, her inner radar will be fully on them. Your greeting will be intrusive because it rips her focus off them and onto you. A tactful nod, wave, or other non-verbal greeting is appropriate in these situations.

It builds lots of people who like espresso and straightforward interactions around blends of option. In addition, the specific tastes of her can show you even regarding her. The typical curiosity is enjoyable and relatable. Outwardly, it is a magnificent spot for a conference. With which observed, be conscious of your frame and surroundings of your time. Several individuals cannot function amicably without their first cup. An additional idea is whether she is en-route to your workplace. Along with the possibility that you think this to become an issue, or perhaps that she is looking forward to what wakes up to the shock of caffeine, it's shrewd to support until sometime shortly.

Attitude of Discovery

Being prepared will cut down on stress so you won't feel so awkward; therefore, you can be yourself. Remember to keep as genuine as possible because, in future times, it will be difficult to keep track of how you acted around her previously.

Besides, your friends will ultimately meet her if you start dating. Your seduction can quickly turn into a humiliating mess if you treat her differently. Sometimes people are not self-aware enough to detect character flaws or irritable habits. If you worry that something is undetectable to you, ask friends or family members for their honest opinion. Self-assessment can be a wonderful process but stressful if attempted with an unknown party. It's much easier to turn an awkward moment into laughter with family and friends rather than to receive harsh analysis from her. She may use humour to break the ice. If that's not your style, don't try to gratify her by pushing yours. Forced humour creates awkwardness. There are vast arrays of characteristics that you can use in place of humour. Refer to whatever music may be playing, wear an authentic smile while inquiring about her tastes. If music is absent and you like to read, ask if she can recommend a good book. Comment on the location if all else fails. To realize similar tastes, tactfully create an attitude of discovery. If an unfamiliar subject is uncovered, feel free to explore it but don't portray yourself as knowing something in which you don't. even if it's a subject in which she expects you to be interested, don't allow her pressure to effectively trap you in a bad situation. In the end, misrepresentation leads to damage control.

Pursue or Walk Away?

Let's reverse to the greeting for a moment; once you've made the first step, she should respond in some fashion. even if the greeting didn't require her to speak, body language is also communication. Stay aware of the expressions of her for indications of approachability (relaxed air) or maybe disregard (any firmness of rejection). Grinning presents a chance to find out hygiene. Did she lean toward you or even out? Did she consider you, past you, or perhaps is her notice darting about? If perhaps she displays some being easily annoyed, you might wish to apologize for your intrusion and exit the situation. argued reactions might mean a misconception or maybe she may need the room.

Should you duplicate yourself and she appears uncertain, decrease it and go on. She will go after the issue from there in case she is engaged. You just don't know, the actual opposite might come about. She may grant you a beautiful smile with a sunny disposition that lights up your senses. When brain cells and physique fire from her surface beauty, you should quickly check for characteristics that you prefer in a woman. That doesn't mean sweep her off her feet and light the candles. This presents a prime opportunity to closely observe her for qualities which attract you. voice timber and laugh alongside expressiveness and attitude play a huge roll in her personality. They'll additionally have an effect on you; thus, influencing the amount of vibe and closeness of the response of yours. In the event that the characteristics aggravate you, rethink settling for her. If perhaps she does grow to be almost everything you have dreamed (or maybe more), continue chatting and keep eye communication. When your focus roams to various other areas only at that stage, she could turn you lower quick. Then, a greater degree of comprehension is talked about determining whether or not she is drawn to you or simply socially responsive generally.

A Deeper Understanding

Usually, a polite greeting or maybe reply will grant you the same. Humanity has a tendency to mirror behaviour if we very first meet up with each other. To appear a little much deeper, we've got to check out truthfulness and find out the path of intention. Her entire body words (movements and expressions alike) would be the secrets. Getting gifts while pinpointing explicit agreeableness or maybe dismissal will work for you in various zones. It's something other than a basic project especially along the way from the possibility that you both have not witnessed her cooperate with others or even have not even collaborated with her until now.

Confidence Standard

If you want to overcome the thinking that women have that men will leave them immediately if they are easy to take to bed, here is what you can tell as a story to put calm and confidence in a woman's mind. Make sure to introduce this natural way in conversation. Wait until you have a "cue" to start saying this. Think of it as a puzzle where you're trying to put one more piece. "Oh yeah, trust ... it's funny. I lost faith in women a few years ago ". Now you need to pause here for her to ask" for what? ". Taking this break you get two things. The first is that you don't spoil your "unrehearsed story" cover by reciting quickly a memorized account. And second is that you may be putting it on perfect position for your intentions. She will want to prove that you are deceived and restore your faith in the confidence of women. "I spent one night with a woman and we didn't see each other for two months of it ". Here you are saying that spending just one night with a woman is good. The way that you are saying this in an open conversation with a woman will dispel the bad thoughts that women have about going through an evening with a man with whom they are not in a relationship. Then say, "I lost her phone number and then I couldn't call her ". Now you're saying that you didn't like most of the men who don't even care about getting what they wanted from the woman. You say you would have called if you hadn't missed the number telephone. It also means that you still want to see the woman after spend a night with her and she'll think, "If I fuck him, he won't leave me afterwards as all other men do. I don't need to give a difficult one with him to keep him interested in me ". You then say: "Well, what occurred was that a good friend of mine come and also directed me in case I'd sex with this particular female ". You're currently setting up the mind of her which you do not head out as well as explain to others regarding the stories of his with females, not near buddies. She is going to think "If he does not head out speaking with the friends of his, he most likely does not speak to no person what he did towards the female ". After that point out, "I could not trust what I was listening to. I in no way I claim, not to the best friends of mine, what I actually do as well as what I do not do with females, therefore it had been most likely she that had reported a thing. At this moment you're acting surprised as well as perplexed at the way the info spread since you do not inform everyone regarding the stories of yours with females.

Rejection

Certain behaviours may signal or hide her rejection. Distraction (constantly checking her phone, purse, or anything nearby) is a signal of her lack of interest. A clear indication is when she tells you that she's waiting for anything (other than the line in which you're standing to move forward). It's her way of alerting you that she's too distracted or busy at the moment. Common sense tells us that a flat no if she walks away, or distaste of any kind is plain rejection. Some people are natural social butterflies (appear tactful and polite at all times). The ability to read involuntary body language is very important. To detect further distraction or falsehoods, notice if she consistently looks away when speaking. Her thoughts may be in direct contrast if she doesn't maintain eye contact or leans away from you even if politely responding to you. It's not a need to be untrue but a protective stance. It might be she does not wish to damage you or perhaps fears mental participation. Whenever a tight rejection comes across, do not allow it to affect you a lot. Realize that many additional females in your range experienced calm and tactful withdrawal from a likely stressed circumstance. Now you've made at least two positive impacts (if not more) within viewing range. even if the original in which you approached thinks she surfaced with the upper hand, you emerge the victor. You never know, the impact may change her mind or cause her to realize that she holds the character flaw. Keep in mind that your true character led them to that conclusion.

Approachability

An interested woman will (most likely) look you in the eye when she meets you. If she doesn't, the reason could be shyness or low self-worth. She will possibly be more receptive upon finding a common interest. Active listening (leaning in or remaining focused) is a positive sign. It shows that your first contact has been a success. She is experiencing the encounter. Right now could be a marvellous moment to think about finding out if she stays in the area for more discussion. In that case, she is curious (in the mind) of yours. Her entire body of words (laying a hand on your arm or even articulating emotion in reaction to that which you mention or even the way you mention it) suggests proactive listening. With that said, don't get the champagne ready just yet. Many times, culture plays a huge role in how she socially interacts. She might lightly hug, brush your shoulder, or give you a peck on the cheek after the first meeting. This customary affection is a compliment saying 'nice to meet you' and should be taken as nothing more. That's not to say that she doesn't have heightened interest in you. Attitude, body language, and various other factors such as the speed of talking distinguish between interest and general body language. Her light brush or hug may be an exuberant need to connect because you share common ground. A wise choice would be to note it for further exploration (at a later time). Rushing it will not get you physically closer to her.

When a polite exchange gives way to conversation, spending too much time talking about one topic (work, sports, etc.) is unfavourable. You need her to supply you with information as well as a company. Pause significantly at the end of each statement to allow for her interaction especially if you are a natural conversationalist. Nerves can also accelerate speech as well as create a need to ramble. If this happens, count to ten to calm your nerves and try to keep the subject focused on one thing at a time.

In chance encounters, always be alert to traffic (people and vehicles) moving around you. even though you may be thrilled at seeing her, the rushed mother of three may find her children willing to run you over. To turn a department or grocery store encounter into a scored phone number, quick thinking and awareness are crucial.

An attentive balance, quickly motioning toward the bustling traffic and brisk access to your mobile phone is required. An expression, for example, "May I call you at some point when we're less occupied?" (or moreover) is suitable. You may get killed be that as it may, at that point you'll know. Then again, your promptly accessible phone will be empowering. She may pull out her phone to log your number without offering hers. If so, feel free to be the perfect gentleman and tactfully ask her to call you right then to verify. It's a clever move and will signal your interest by supplying her with your number. It's not considered bullying because you've asked due to a busy area. There was no ill intent. Although Twitter and instant messaging usernames may be forthcoming, reluctance to provide social networking information is normal. Because of the significant amount of information provided on these sites, protective behaviour is much more common. Nonetheless, the exchange of numbers moves you a step closer to your goal.

To begin with Dates and Such

When you come across a female initially and use tips to the advantage of yours mental, the organic outcome may be the waking up of specific curiosity of her for you, and the readiness to reach understand you much more. Teach yourself to be a fun type, not requiring herself to be way too real, serious about herself and her things and that knows how to tune in carefully. You're not really frantic in style, however, you allow a while to go by just before labelling her so a unique moment prior to going away with her on a particular date initially, and the moment arrived. These measures function not just on this very first day but on every consequential what about the following conferences? She has an expert opinion of you and also the hardest part of a great perception is generating it, keeping it simple in case you bolster that favourable first opinion in subsequent meetings of yours. The most significant factor is losing dread and being crystal clear in your actions and words, though she's constantly identified it, nowadays it's entirely sharp which your interest in here It's a loving connection and also in case she's had you it's since she additionally wishes identical with you, therefore do not hesitate. Laugh, appear to be her within the eye, contact her, question her concerning the experiences of her in like preventing on the good versions and therefore you will associate them along with you, and discuss sex with complete protection to ensure she can feel self-confident and also dares to speak about it along with you without being sorry. This is his moment, though it is you that has the influence, the nighttime can conclude within a fantastic erotic sexual encounter, or perhaps with the start of a courtship, that depends upon you and everything you need, think me: she's entirely under your control.

People tend to act their best during face-to-face scenarios; therefore, the person with whom you spoke might seem more relaxed within the privacy offered through technology. You should wait at least a full day before you attempt to contact. Let her think about you. If things went well in the first meeting, you shouldn't doubt her interest you will be on her mind. It will be easier to get to know her after you allow a little time to pass. You shouldn't wait longer than the third day. After that, she may shrug you off. You should remember that that in case you discover you're not agreeable within every stage, it's suggested to returned at bay.

even if the attraction is purely physical and you don't plan on a relationship. A discovery of nothing in common or lack of sparks or interest on either behalf should signal you to drop the plan. Continuation will lead to hard feelings on either of your behalf. When to Call, Text, or IM Unless she leaves her wallet at the location where you met, don't contact her immediately. If something similar does happen, quickly call her. Otherwise, discomfort or suspicion may result even if you just want to say hi. Avoid overt interest or coming across needy. If she calls you, get ready to start picking her mind for clues. Let's say that she doesn't call you. Once the initial meeting and information have been exchanged and you've confirmed your attraction, you shouldn't wait too long before asking her out. On the other hand, moving faster than a full day creates the wrong vibe. Anything sooner than 24 hours will make her wonder why you need her to occupy your time. This starts a snowball of negative notions. On that third day, she starts thinking you lack interest. You don't want her forgetting you or thinking she's a low priority within your world. During these two days, think about tactful ways to obtain information. Whatever you get will determine your first date.

If you want to have excellent results the key is: Do not give too much importance. This contradicts the traditional idea which establishes that you must go to every appointment on time, even be before the specified time and wait there, take care excessively your appearance, being excessively chivalrous and educated avoiding saying or doing anything that might offend her, give her a beautiful bouquet and a box of the finest chocolates; in short, make your first date a beautiful, romantic and cheesy moment.

Repeat Discovery Process

First dates (similar to first impressions) require planning. gain information the same way you navigated through your first meeting. You have permission to call her so now transfer the same discovery process you used in the meeting to get information for a first date. Use your interests as a guide to starting brainstorming. In this early stage of contact, you will discover her normal routine (work, college, etc.). These items will allow you to cater to her schedule and suggest an event that's designed for her. By tailoring the entire date, you will greatly impress her. An additional consideration is required. Does she have children or an elderly relative that require a sitter? If so, she may need a back-up plan. If you offer assistance with this process, it will score tremendous points. Whatever the outcome, allow her extra time to arrange and maintain patience throughout. Search for many things and compile a list. You shouldn't settle for the first thing she says because she might just be thinking out loud. Your aim should be a well-rounded, thoughtful evening meant to impress. Find out what places she yearns to visit, the food she loves, and offer to go into the city or country for an adventure. explore something different but make sure it's something you both enjoy. Scour the area for new restaurants or see if she likes the beach (if you're within a close distance). Once you've established easy conversation through technology, something important to inquire early on is if she likes noisy places. You could ask her about loud music. Is she allergic to animals, any types of flowers or food? You may want to send her flowers at some point and need to avoid restaurants serving items in which she's allergic. Are there any sports she likes? What types of movies? This is a crucial one. You may find a love for cuddling in front of movies with popcorn but be careful. The movie along with the extent of cuddling should be agreeable to you both. If her taste in movies doesn't coincide with yours, viewing could be unpleasant for both and all snuggling will vanish. Remember, the movie first and then cuddling (in her mind). If you don't like tearjerkers, don't agree to one. Both of you might be frowning by the end. Instead of translating a desire to be with your date, she'll think you attended just for the contact. even if you did, she doesn't need to know that at this point. Similarly, don't promise something that you cannot deliver. If she's always wanted to sail on a yacht, agree about your common idea regarding fun fantasies and move on to lesser expensive thoughts. If she announces access to a log cabin with promises to cook you a fine meal, make sure you offset with an appropriate response and gift (have her offer suggestions on wine). You'll discover if she drinks, her tastes in wine, and (if she doesn't) the question can lead to other pertinent interests. This brings to mind a relevant question: "What about asking for payment to cover her portion?" The best course of action would be to pay for the entire date if you've set it up. She could surprise you (be very independent) and offer to pay half or pick up for the next date. How can you think regarding her paying out the way of yours or even remaining impartial? Finding she's impartial might be a great idea. She's showing a preference for paying her way and could be searching for someone in which to share. In case she doesn't offer, bring enough to pay for both. If she is independent, she could request to drive herself to the location. If so, make sure she suggests the location. If you have any anxiety over it, prepare a map or develop your route beforehand. If you pick her up, tactfully inquire if others will be present at the location. She may want someone else to meet you so she can get an opinion before the date. even though common sense states to look appropriate, the personal dress should be touched on as well. Avoid overdressing or spraying on heavy cologne. Being in an enclosed place trapped with overwhelming aroma might quickly end the evening. Of course, ripped jeans and a T-shirt (unless appropriate) shouldn't be worn. Shaving is recommended because you never know how close you may get. The sensitive skin under rough facial hair is not pleasant and, unless you've already discussed it, she may not like facial hair. Also, don't forget to let her know if any specific dress code is required of her. Always keep in mind the limited interaction you've had with her. Throughout, you should remain genuine. Also, be aware of how she acts. Nervousness is one thing but she should portray herself in a balanced fashion. While getting to know one another, keep it simple and relaxed. If you appear with a different persona each time, she'll wonder if you're trying to make her uncomfortable. Precisely the same is true for her. When you discover she uses a unique disposition every time you speak, it might signify she is not pleased with the communication.

MOVING FORWARD
Face-to-Face

There is no simple procedure to guarantee the main date goes easily. Once you've gathered enough data, set the occasion moving and attempt to take advantage of whatever occurs. By this point, you ought to know about her character enough to fill in the spaces during and after this next meeting. The basic principle goal is growing to be a lot more familiar with each other inside an interpersonal environment. Hold with mind… go gradually and also permit her to put the firmness. During your time with her, use that discovery process once again to acquire missing pieces. You'll principally have an impressive deal to uncover about roughly one another. At this point, don't worry about what may happen in the future. Instead, concentrate on getting to know her to recognize compatibility and strengthen your connection. Physical contact such as a kiss to top it off would solely depend on vibes throughout the evening. Only attempt if you're sure she's accepting or she gives you a distinctly clear invitation to go ahead (otherwise it's risky). She may surprise you and initiate contact. At this point, let her set all physical levels.

If the event's outcome leaves you pleasantly anticipating seeing each other again, you know you're headed in the right direction. If it turns negative, you can always try again. It's not too late yet. More intimacy can be expected because your comfort zone strengthened by finding common interests. Continue to keep the interaction moving forward in this time. Busting it right now or even altering abruptly leads to needless misunderstandings. Each of you needs to count on another particular date while ongoing to find out about one another.

The following date ought to be similarly as

one of a kind as the first however extraordinary at a similar time. Since you know each other better, you may put your inventive abilities together to conceptualize for the following gathering. If she needs it to be amazement, dazzle her concerning the amount you as of now think about her. Along the way from possibility you, despite every negligible thing end up in a misfortune, prudently try letting her understand that you require proposals. Attempt to bargain and enable info about her. If she is not gratifying, swear through the revelation process or even locate help at companions.

Tips for Owning the experience

Regarding previous dates and locations, you shouldn't avoid them with her but make sure your previous dates don't frequent the same places. It would also be awkward if you know people that have seen you with previous dates at specific areas. Ask around or scout these places out before attending with her. enlist your friends' help with sorting them out and then get advice on a list of new places. More than one friend (possibly their girlfriends separately) needs to be accessed to get a well-rounded view of what areas have to offer. The following are tips on gaining more information, determining interest level, and offer activities that are easy on bank accounts: even though some things are important to know, don't ask straightforward questions similar to, "Are you good at hand-on activities?" These phrases are loaded with implied meaning. Sure, they might spur mental activity along the same lines as you but she might not be ready for that course of thinking. If not, she'll shut you down quickly. To find out something similar, ask in a roundabout way. For example, has she ever taken any courses (pottery or jewellery-making, cake decorating, flower arranging, etc....geared toward hands-on involvement)? This doesn't mean you've agreed to bake a cake. It's a tactful way to discover if she's willing to learn new things and gives you an idea of what she's already explored. Tip: it is a very good sign if she intently watches your hands while you create something. Brainstorm on similar classes (appealing to both of you) and check availability in your area. Do you live in a rural region or the city? Check out horse riding through the country. Hire a stroll in a horse-drawn carriage if available. Sometimes the more satisfying dates are less costly because no one is worried about expenses. The word 'free' will aptly describe both your attitudes because it wipes away stress, cost, and pressure. This factor makes that walk on the beach more relaxing, building a snowman more thrilling, and volunteering for whatever even more rewarding. It also gives you a sense of unity or teamwork. You should pay close attention to how the two of you socially mesh. Speaking of social contact, she could range from exuberant to withdrawn. Keep in mind that people will protect themselves in groups or crowds; therefore, inadvertently wearing a mask. However, you may stumble upon a child at heart. A theme park offering roller coasters and chances to win oversized stuffed animals could be just the thing. Is she intellectual or artistic? If so, explore a local museum or art gallery.

Thrifty? Beaches and sunshine aren't the only conditions suitable for fresh air. Dependent upon the time of year, holiday lights may be viewable. Take a walk through the city after dark or drive through some decorated neighbourhoods. Halloween is a ticket for the inner child in all of us to run wild. If she loves that time of year, take her to a haunted house. There are parties to attend, pumpkins to carve, or colourful tree-lined routes to take if she's not fond of scare tactics. Tip for creating a sensory memory: impress her by coating pumpkin seeds with a sprinkle of salt, spice (BBQ, chilli powder, nutmeg, etc.), or cinnamon and sugar. Bake: single-layered on a non-stick pan at 325°C for 10 minutes (turn over an additional 10 minutes or until crispy). When she eats or smells whatever spice you used (afterwards), your memory will surface. Plus, it's a very health-conscious holiday snack. even if she doesn't want to try them, the thoughtful gesture (amid lingering aromas of spice) will still cause the desired impact. If either of you can cook, see if she wants to help prepare dinner one night. It will give you both a chance to see how the other operates within a kitchen. Let's say that you cook but she doesn't. Show her how to prepare the previous simple recipe and teach her some simple kitchen skills. Plus, you can go shopping for the supplies and find out tastes, attitude, and level of stress she carries within a public environment.

If neither of you cooks, just keep the tip in mind to establish the memories through other routes. Strong aromas and tastes create bookmarks in our minds. You shouldn't go overboard and make sure she likes the aroma or taste. All of these things influence future dates so you might as well find them out early. By today, posts uncovered an understanding of favourites and sports. She might even get involved in a single but do not hurry to interact with her within the play. Seeing any sporting activity initially will give you a good grasp of her level of expertise and allow you to recognise which teams she favours. Then question her for a living occasion in case you love similar teams. Another category (frequently ignored opportunity) is house maintenance. Nearly all individuals do not take care of maintenance as whatever, aside from an obligation. Change it right into several dates. If your relationship is at that flirtatious sparking point, you may find anticipation for upcoming shopping trips. A tip: playfully initiate discussions (sparing use of implications) regarding purchases. See if it takes you anywhere. If not, you tried. Now you know she's not ready. If she's game, offer to help (or have her help) and keep that anticipation going through continued communication. Parks are another easily ignored source. Find a cosy place under a tree for a picnic or a bench to watch people walk their dogs and children play. Watching people brings out an interest in humanity, which gives you a window on her opinions regarding the world. Gazing at the night sky is another option. If this appeals, schedule time for an evening picnic and eat under the stars or during a full moon. You never know, you may witness a shooting star. If she's into cosmology, take her to an observatory and see a film on the creation of the universe.

Some Rules to Remember

As you get more relaxed around her, don't forget good manners. Be patient if she still wants to drive herself on the second date. Always maintain good hygiene throughout this time because you never know what may happen. Remain alert and prepared while keeping your connection through phone and digital formats but don't flood her with attention and messages.

The more data you gather, the simpler it will be to set up the second what's more, resulting dates. When you've perceived how she works socially, you ought to have the option to tell whether she'll coexist with your loved ones. Think about a twofold date or gathering for future occasions if she's willing.

After the Second Date

Asking her to stick around for some after-date time is acceptable. It shows her that you are enjoying the date and want to extend the time you spend with her. Offering to go for drinks is an easy way to do this. Keep preferences that you already know about her in mind when asking. The lengthy proposal shouldn't be for beverages inside whether residence plus it does not need to be alcohol or coffee. Your best bet would be attending a public place with a wide variety of drink and food. Why? She may be hungry again. Sometimes, people are reluctant to ask for something on a date. She may feel that she's intruding or you'll think she eats too much. Most women are notoriously worried about their appearance and never want to appear as if they overeat. She will also be more comfortable eating and making decisions within a restaurant. even if it's relatively late, diners or 24-hour restaurants serve a variety of drinks and desserts. Along with the way from the possibility that she will take you in place along the offer, you should not recognize that she will permit additional events to happen. Again, allow her to establish firmness. Contingent upon what it has incorporated within the day (loud organizations, having flatware banging, therefore on.), this might present a primary period for fixation. Focus on getting a lot more familiar with each other. Breaks in the conversation can be problematic or awkward. When you encounter a pause, ask her about herself. If she works, explore that route. If you already know where she works and all about her job, ask questions based on that knowledge. Why did she choose that career? Any college and do you have college experience for comparison? Smooth communication can turn into a lengthy discussion involving funny stories and childhood memories. explore all appropriate topics but keep heavy subjects (religion, politics, sex, etc.) out of it until you know her better.

Things to Consider

If she refuses any after-date time, don't worry. She may have to work the next day or the sitter could be waiting. There's a possibility she wants to take things slow because of personal experience. Recognize that your offer relates your fun and effectively sends a signal of your continued desire for contact. That's what counts. Besides your company, drink, and possible food; don't imply availability on other fronts. If she playfully inquires about your expectations, don't offer them even if your tongue is on fire. Dampen your tongue with whatever current drink you're enjoying and show heightened respect for her. If this does happen, she just let you know that she's intrigued. Please be aware that her intrigue will hold.

Also remain alert to the possibility that if you jump now, she may not continue further communication. Realize that you're on her mind and be patient because sharp anticipation benefits both of you. In comparison with true fire, this early blaze smothers easily when fanned too soon. Throw fuel to it and it may get out of control. If you want something lasting, check yourself and hold off.

Are We There Yet?

Having formed a bond with her that holds sparks, you now must be patient. If things are still moving forward, your connection is there on some level. Start planning for more dates. Try different locations and times since you know her schedule better. If you had a candle-lit restaurant dinner last time, try meeting for a picnic lunch at the park this time. However, you can actually shift from meals as the key design. Try a more active route like rock climbing. It's normal for you to excessively think about her. Try not to bombard her too much because she may already feel overwhelmed. By now, you should know her sense of humour well enough to send her a joke or two by text but be careful not to send her something specifically inappropriate (sending photos of self [sexting], etc.).

After the second date, you'll want to attempt to increase the intimacy in your communication regardless of whether you've been physical in any way. Flirtatious or provocative replies will signal her thoughts along the same route. Any flirting response on your part is playful teasing and required at this point. You want to keep that anticipation humming in the background. Without it, you become good friends. You should wait for the subject to come up or tactfully lead into it. Contrary to popular belief, most women are just as leery of commitment as men. If the subject does arise, you may find that wedding bells are not ringing in her mind. Don't take it personally. just as you probably feel, she's searching and resistant to settling too fast. At this point, some may see this as a challenge. Don't take her reserved attitude personally. Understand that, after talk of this nature, she may feel just as vulnerable. Pressuring her into something in which she's not ready will send her running. She may be dating others, too. Ignore it and them. If you don't, her instincts will scream for her to leave you alone. If she wants to know if you're seeing others, be completely honest. If she gets mad, talk it through. As stated before regarding yourself, allow her to choose you amongst whomever she's dating. As long as an open flow of communication along with the anticipation to see each other again is present, you shouldn't have a problem. Be aware of her and your feeling at all times, though, and make sure you remain completely open with her.

Finding a different suitor is usually basic. Keep in mind, however, she is nonetheless viewing you consequently there has to be a little something regarding you which draws in her. It is the job of yours to learn what as well as ensure you stay sexy. Should you start to be furious in the additional dates, you are going to become the problem of her rather than the possible mate of her. Anything you do, do not take upwards commitment or marriage. She will receive a bad impact.

That Intimate Moment

When you reach the linen division for which ultra-soft group of sheets, don't forget that a kiss doesn't result in a receptive bedroom doorstep. For all that you understand, she is a careless kisser having a horrid inhale. On that mention, you need to reach for the kiss. As previously stated, intimacy should be a shared intention by the third date. You should know by now what she considers romantic. even so, you may want to ask female relatives or maybe your friends have companions that will help. gestures that appear romantic to some may look tacky to others so you want to have an idea of her tastes before you make plans. By this time, your hormones have probably gotten some aspects of you in an uproar. Try to focus on the romance versus the end goal of sex. Bringing flowers may seem a bit outdated but, if she loves a beautiful bouquet, take her to a huge garden. Tip: Avoid buying roses this early because their specific colours imply intent and feelings. Location and atmosphere of date are very important. Drag racing and football are not preferable. Neither are tempting places she may be required to change clothing (like the beach). For your peace of mind, avoid swimsuits until after you've spent more time in each other's presence. Romance is about setting the mood and relaying that you're highly interested in the overall package. That doesn't mean you're forecasting the attitude of 'Hey, I want to get you into my bed!' Though it will try letting her recognize you would like to get it one step further. Keep in mind that 'further' (from her mind) might be an impressive deal, the same as the edition in your mind. Have a shot at preparing romantic movements which put her inside a far calmer condition plus, in exactly the same period, provide her with complete attention of yours.

Ideas and Suggestions

Many previously listed romantic gestures include moonlit picnics, walks on the beach, and candlelight dinners (obvious choices). Truthfully, anything can be romantic. There are plenty of activities in which to choose. A trip with wine tasting at a vineyard may be a good choice if you share similar tastes. A rooftop or waterside view of the sunset or sunrise is something everyone enjoys. If she loves candy, schedule a tour with a candy factory. As long as you give her total focus, she'll feel your interest. If your budget is tight, a planned walk along the right nature trail (maybe with a waterfall) can be perfect. City lights viewed from just the right rooftop or even watching the sunset from inside a tall building can have the desired impact. Of course, the romance will influence you as well. Your mind (like hers) will be on that first intimate contact. Try not to let anxiety make you edgy. To remain stress-free, you should make sure that you've prepared yourself. Your lack of nerves will portray confidence, which will influence her level of participation.

Notwithstanding your normal sanitation (shower, antiperspirant, tooth locks, therefore on.), you will need to shave. Along with being away from possibility, you have not merely discovered after the kiss will function as the 2nd to produce a feeling of along the off chance which she brains skin locks. Restrict cologne. You'll be not able to smell it since your faculties have grown accustomed to that fragrance. Everybody else scents it. Clothing should be appropriate. She's going to be standing close so avoid wool or scratchy material. A heavily starched shirt is another thing to avoid. If she lays a hand on your arm, chest, or shoulder; she doesn't want to feel cardboard. Most woman will lay a hand somewhere when they're being kissed so consider wearing a soft shirt. Tip: bring breath mints or chewing gum. Not only will it sweeten your breath, but it will also help with a dry mouth (if nerves hit). Candy is helpful, too, but crunching it all night might be disturbing to her. Any health issue (even a common cold, allergies, or a cold sore) should delay the entire date. You do not wish to produce her ill. Also, the strain will irritate and also your chance of turning out to be much more sick which hampers each improvement.

The Kiss

Both of you are expecting it so (rest assured) the kiss will happen. You'll need to be within her physical range so stay nearby but don't make it completely obvious. There will be a moment when eye contact or leaning in of one (or both) will prompt it. Your heads will tilt to avoid bumping noses before your lips touch each other. This is another instance where she must lead the way. At this point, her vulnerability shows up again. You may want to deepen it but wait. Moving too fast will have her backing off. If she initiates the heat, let her keep control. She may some show urgency. In that case, don't let her cross whatever lines you've drawn. Arousal (on either part) is completely normal. You've just spent however amount of time getting to know her. It's natural for you to take it to the next step. Nevertheless, keep your hands on her cheeks, hair or shoulders. You are discovering boundaries in which she's silently defining. Your fingers may want to climb down her arms but this kiss will stick in her mind if you keep it simple and follow her lead. Anything added and she'll focus on the added touch versus the building of anticipation meant by the kiss. By now, you should know her feelings regarding a man who takes charge. even if she claims she does, most women don't appreciate it on that first kiss.

Seduction is a gradual procedure. According to her personality, hurrying towards the surface type can make midsections seem minor. While it will surely go far today, it breaks the powerful interconnection off. Rational sex action with happy recollections is all that stays for her. Because of this specific, there might not be another photo at whatever.

Your Place

Around the third date, visits to one another's homes will no doubt occur (if not as of now). She'll see things for which you ought to plan. Even though it might be marginally upsetting, careful cleaning is altogether. Decorate, the right ambience is important for seduction. Attempt to determine the feelings with two accessories. Candles, and feelings burning, can help you move a lot. Once you drop by the foundation with a female initially, she could really feel insecure. Dimming the lightweight and illuminating several candles might really help her feel much more comfortable when she requires the above. We may also regard candles as exciting and romantic by several. Try tidying upwards slightly in advance. A magnificent house that is clean can allow you to appear gathered up and conscientious, that converts on women that are many.

Tip: inquire as to whether she has hypersensitivities to pets or cleaning things like fragrant cover powder. On the off chance that spending plan permits, enlist expert assistance. Ask a family part or companion to help in case you're on a strict financial plan or need time.

Pick scents to the advantage of yours. If you let a female of for you, an enjoyable fragrance is vital to seduction. Attempt to always keep the house windows receptive for a couple working hours to ensure that any kind of undesirable fragrance evaporates. Light a few scented candles. Opt for a pleasant aroma that is not too penetrating, such as a light vanilla scent or sandalwood. Try to find out which scent you like in advance. For example, you can include questions about fragrances in a conversation. For example, ask her about the types of perfumes she likes to wear or body lotions she uses to get an idea of which scents she prefers. Similar to body sprays and deodorants, specific aromas escape our noses when consistently around them. The same applies to your living space. Have someone walk through and sniff-test to see if the cleaning was thorough enough. Similarly, ask the same person to alert you (after an extended stay) to any irritations like noisy neighbours or their pets. You may share a love for animals and sports cars but the loud odour of pets or screaming of a car alarm could put a damper on your evening. If other people reside with you, have them make plans or stay in one specific area (if you choose to wait on introductions). Offering something in return to the other party should help them to understand (a favour for a favour). For pets, try to keep them separate until you understand how your furry friend will react to her. She may be thrilled and own pets herself. On that mention, ensure you allow her to recognize should you experience allergy symptoms to anything at all.

At her arrival, cater to her. If she brings a gift, graciously accept no matter what it is. Ask if she wants a drink. Point out the proper placement of purse, coat, shoes, or umbrella. Avoid having her place her belongings somewhere out of the main space. At no point, should you manoeuvre her toward your bedroom? even if you're giving a tour of the place, motion in the direction if you must but don't go near it. Stepping into that space will cause awkwardness that is detrimental right now.

A movie is a good frame of time for her to relax in your surroundings; yet, not cause your sequestered roommate or pet to go completely stir-crazy. If you do pick a movie, check the rating and content. When it gets overly steamy or horrific, she might think you tried to set her up. You should (of course) remove all provocative materials. even if the nude art of on your wall is a significant expression of self, remove it until you get to know her a little better. The clock that makes you chuckle every time you check the time might make her cringe. video games can be explored but don't scream at the TV too loud. Your new hot game could be a bit raunchy just yet. That is unless she's yelling right along with you and proving herself a worthy teammate when shooting zombies to save tomorrow. If you discover ignorance for gaming, see if she likes cards or board games. Most local thrift stores have an abundance of them. Possibly pick up a meal at a drive-through or order a pizza for delivery. If you're really in the mood to shop, stop at the grocery store and buy enough to jointly prepare a meal. You may be able to impress her with some outdoor cooking skills on the grill.

Her Place

Visiting her private areas may show a previously hidden side of her. If this happens and you discover someone that is not compatible, a friendship instead of seduction may need considering. Regardless, you should treat her residence similarly and avoid her bedroom. If asked over to her place, a gift is a thoughtful gesture. Base your selection on what you already know of her tastes. Pick something that compliments any home (flowers, wine, or even her blend of coffee). Avoid candles unless you know she prefers a specific scent. Another gift area to avoid is anything regarding her beliefs (even if you've attended her church). Rules may apply in her specific area such as parking, noise control, etc. When entering her home, check to see if shoe placement is by the door. If so, remove yours and leave them there. Be alert to weather conditions. You don't want to track snow, mud, or leave a wet trail behind you. Ask where to place muddy items or umbrella and raincoat.

Also, pay attention to her specific comfort zones. Wear and tear signify favourite seats. Choose a different spot. No matter what, do not place your feet on her furniture. Your awareness and consideration will stand out. If she's preparing a meal, ask if she needs help. Don't insist if she says everything is under control. If you do participate in an activity such as dinner, ask afterwards if she needs assistance with cleaning. Your willingness to help will leave an impression even if your help is not required.

Merging Comfort Zones

Finding joint comfort in each other's surroundings can be a heady experience. The bond that you've formed will strengthen as more time passes within each of your homes. Keep this in mind when either of you is visiting. Above all, be patient. You don't want to push bedroom intimacy too fast. With that said, avoid becoming so content that you leave clutter or lapse into untidiness within your home. She may drop by unexpected and experience shock at what she thought was to be her retreat. Opening up to share deeper tastes is normal. Don't break out the scariest movies, though. She will notice your respect at such. Use the discovery process to explore deeper tastes but through communication. A trip to a local video store together will show similar tastes. Tip: finger snacks like popcorn or candy can benefit you regarding amplifying anticipation. Eating is a shared activity that can prompt playfulness and desire. Many types of food can be sexy. Think adventurous and romantic verses blunt behaviour. Several subtle moves are ranging from feeding her a bite off your silverware to eating popcorn from the palm of her hand. You should remain alert to several opportunities (based on your level of connection). Regarding that tantalizing smear of sauce, you should move toward a napkin instead of using a thumb-to-tongue technique. Don't expect her to eat popcorn out of your hand as well.

Together with the collection, subtly suggestive treats including chocolate-covered strawberries alongside champagne will be an enjoyable romantic treat. I will integrate meals like oysters into the supper but ensure she wants them initially. This is not a time to fulfil fantasies or maybe experience ironic occasions (even through playful dares).

Love Seat or Sofa?

Even if you're happy conversing over after-dinner coffee at the kitchen table, suggest moving to the sofa for music or to watch a movie. The sofa is a perfect place to kiss, pet, or just cuddle. Tip: she's still experiencing a build of anticipation. Become creative with petting and cuddling to advance that anticipation without crossing the line. You want her to mirror your actions. Leaning toward her while sitting closely will prompt cuddling. By now, this action signals intent to share space to enjoy her nearness. If she feels the same, she'll move closer. Your end goal may be showing your appreciation on a mattress but (first) get her accustomed to your physical presence through other means. You might try messaging a hand or her feet. Running your fingers through her hair (at the back), a neck massage, or playing with an earring will make her feel special. If this is acceptable, move to her shoulders (clothes remaining on bodies) or gently rub her back if she leans forward. She may turn toward you, lean into you, or any number of accepting responses. Your expression of attraction crosses into possible petting and light caresses (hugs and kisses included) at this point. Touching the back of her torso needs to be welcome and appropriate. Do not advance lower or around to her front unless she moves you there or verbally asks you to go there. Urging any part of her into your lap (feet not included) should be treated in the same fashion. Snuggling or cuddling is light foreplay. Nevertheless, don't think it over being a certain beneficial for hurrying to the sheets. At any point, she might back off. Show respect for her if she does at any point. Also, don't allow her to push you into anything in which you are uncomfortable. This type of touching will create a hormonal response; thus, leading to further relaxation, strengthened connections, and a serene feeling for both of you.

Transition into heavier play is entirely possible. Amplified arousal through deep kisses and petting is to be expected. You may discover a difficulty to keep your hands off each other. While clothing remains intact, heightened pleasure and possible fulfilment can be reached. In other words, these actions are beneficial but your bedroom moves need to be kept secret for now. If sexual heat reaches a boiling point, consider this: stick to the couch and concentrate on pleasing her through caresses and fondling. Hands can do besides every other section of the body of yours. Undressing specific regions might be needed but do not go all the paths. If you haven't discussed birth control or STDs, you're at a disadvantage but this may prompt those conversations (afterwards). For the time being, stay safe and protected by avoiding the exchange of sexual bodily fluids. Pay attention to what turns her on. Don't depend on past experiences because each woman is different. If breathing doesn't change, pulse accelerates, or no movement is presented; change directions. If she's not moving her hands, she may not be at the same point as you. If she's doing something irritating to you, tactfully let her know by moving her hand to a more desirable location. Just because you're not verbally talking or texting, doesn't mean you're not communicating. It means you've entered the ultimate level of discovery. The more responses gained, the closer you are to understanding her needs. To dance between the sheets, you're required to know her ultimate desires and her to know yours. Don't whisper your most in-depth fantasies into her ear just yet, though. You want her to be comfortable with you, not feel vulnerable and anxious because she thinks her performance is less than stellar right then. Stay spontaneous while keeping that level of anticipation moving forward.

Sexual fulfilment (an orgasm) is normal and may happen. As stated earlier, avoid contact with bodily fluids. She may reach a peak before you but, if not, keep moving forward to please her. This can be tricky. Based on her personality type as well as the strength of your connection, you may be able to gain her help (subtly). Tip: move her hand (along with yours) while telling her to show you, and then watch what she does. Some men allow ego to rule at this point, denying the fact that every woman's level of pleasure is different. She won't think you lack sexual knowledge or moves but will appreciate your sensitivity to her specific needs.

If you think your bond is strong but she presents attitude, you just learned she's immature with little to no sense of self. In that case, drop your relationship back into the friend zone (if possible). Otherwise, back out of the seduction. Most likely she is not self-aware; therefore, is accustomed to using others in her discovery of self. If her climaxing is the result, rest assured that you have won her complete attention. A show of gentleness would be to call to assure her safe arrival home. The emotional impact of that level (for her) will vary. She may feel especially vulnerable, connected, or in such a state of anticipation that she can't think straight. Your call will settle that impact into a nice glow until your next meeting.

LET'S ROCK AND ROLL

Now that you've spent a however amount of time discovering what makes each other tick and creating memories, you're ready for the next level.

The proper time for bedtime play has arrived. If the last chapter proved correct, she knows you can please her. Allow no doubt that you are consistently on her mind. You still need to make every effort to impress for that first round of sex. After all, you just spent a lengthy time wooing her. Talk regarding shelter from pregnancy right now. You must understand one another sufficiently that it will not provide some awkwardness or maybe embarrassment. while in case she is in birth management, I advise condoms and STDs are important to become talked about. This area tends to cause vagueness in people. They don't mean to mislead but the embarrassment factor tips the scales. Because of this, a condom is always the smartest decision. Tip: ask if she's allergic to latex.

Again, active listening is the key. Similar to that first date, this event will set a tone for future sessions. Not every location and piece of information that could assist you in setting up a memorable occasion. If taking place within your home, set the mood. Anticipation has been built so regard this next step as if you're wrapping a gift for her. Similar to a birthday, you now need to prepare the atmosphere. Skip the fancy cake and create a party for two. Fragrances such as jasmine can heighten sexuality. we often use Lavender products as a supply of rest. We may buy each at several places. They can be sprayed onto bed sheets or use dried potpourri to freshen the air. Numerous manufacturers use lavender in laundry soap and softener sheets as well. If you're cooking a meal in your home, spices can add to sexual tension. A previous chapter mentioned cinnamon but sensual spices include ginger and basil. Food has also been touched on. Along with chocolate and oysters, avocadoes and asparagus have been known to heighten libido response.

Initiate the first touch.

Begin with the contacts. Once you begin the very first contact, go gradually. Shift from her and include your hand on her shoulder or knee. Soon after: Seduction is about correct velocity. When you go way too rapidly, it can power it down. A major kiss ought to be fine, much more a short-lived kiss compared to a tongue kiss. You need to yearn for extras. Attempt to look at their style. Exactly how might she kiss you too? This could provide you with a signal of what she likes. If you would like to attract a female you have been with for some time, attempt to undertake it inside a surprising manner and in unanticipated spots. Couples easily become routine in long relationships, which can be very boring. For example, try stimulating a tech quack with your wife or girlfriend in the kitchen or the shower.

Maintaining Anticipation

Even though sex is the main event, build up the night so that everything leads in that direction. Numerous activities trigger hormonal responses so that both of you will feel the most impact. Suggest writing each other a heated letter between dates and then reading them to each other on the next date. Or read a light erotic book. Avoid the heavy stuff because they may contain fetish play or roughness which is misleading. Text heated messages between meetings to keep that anticipation brewing. You may want to avoid sending photos and watch language (heavy sexting) due to the possibility of employment issues. Always keep in mind that whatever digital format used, the information may fall into the wrong hands.

Setting the Mood

As the third meeting of yours was targeted toward romance, this conference must be equally (if not more) specific. Every pastime which was also precarious for earlier dates must be examined right now. Listed here are several suggestions: in case of environmental permits, gentle a flame in case you have the heart to ensure you can cuddle close by. A movie that you might have passed over due to content could be appropriate now. Just make sure that she helps pick it out. There may be memories attached that you don't need surfacing while she's with you. Certain foods prove sensual but consider the messy cleanup before buying chocolate sauce, whipped cream, or flavored glaze. Specialty shops offer a wide variety of edible and flavored oils. A warm body massage with scented oil or lotion can quickly move things along. Watching the ocean or taking a moonlit swim (if you live nearby or have access) is another relaxing and sensual experience. Securing a place with a hot tub or even just sinking with her into a bubble bath. Take a shower together. For that matter, a shower before and after may strengthen your connection even more. Tip: Engage her in that sport now (if both athletic) to get your blood pumping and then ask her or offer help washing her back.

Use Sex Stories to Get You Excited

Use your sexual fantasies or experiences to buy the female fired up. By no means make use of accounts specifically affecting the female you're with Speaking. Title everything you did with various females or perhaps what you'd want doing, or perhaps talk to what she's completed with some other males, or even what the friends of her have caused or even what her friends have caused. You are able to utilize it in day interactions, elaborating the design during the appropriate period what about the path particular. Remember that taking the conversation to a sexual mood does not mean necessarily talk explicitly about sex. You can also simply suggest sex by inserting some key sexual words into the conversation (ex: "penetrate", "enjoy", "hard", "ecstasy" used in others senses other than to describe sexual acts or organs). Use your linguistic qualities to say, without actually having to say, what would you like to do with it. Tell a thing within the 3rd individual to indicate what you would like to do with it rather than chatting straight. Example: You say: "I have a friend named Paulo who was telling me what a friend of his did in a nightclub. The guy arrived at the woman, looked at us her eyes and said "I want to eat you all. You want to fuck me". She was shocked by it and almost spilt the drink. But soon after she began to feel a strong excitement and that uncontrollable desire appearing in her body. You know what this feeling of desire is like, right? In be all excited? She was not intimidated and entered the game saying "Only if you suck me first ..." Many women love the romantic and emotional way, while others do not are necessarily interested in a relationship, but in a moment of pure sexual pleasure, without compromises.

So, how do you start talking about these sexual relationships? Well, if you see that she does not respond to emotional and romantic conversation, go beyond this. Offer a different perspective. You can comment as a relationship without commitments can be good, without fights, discussions simply a purely sexual experience between two people. They can experience many things that can be taboo for people in relationships, etc. You can comment on how easy it can be to start something and watch it grow from there when what matters is only physical pleasure. You can say that both men and women, can experiment with their sexual needs and curiosities without any type of insecurities or jealousies in a relationship. on one purely physical relationship, everything is about what makes us feel good and nothing else, exploring fantasies and feeling comfortable with who we are, the way we are.

If you "hit the target", she will agree with you and feel a connection between you because she will feel that you and she are very similar. Now you can ask her what her favourite sexual position is, or the fantasies of hers that she never managed to fulfil in a relationship conventional and closed. You are able to inform about several of the fantasies of yours as well as steer the chat to exactly how great it's to have the ability to exhibit yourself in that way.

Your Bedroom or Hers?

If neither has seen each other's bedroom, you should make sure yours is ready. Commonly overlooked areas such as underneath your bed, ceiling corners, and even darkened closets can hold cobwebs, dust bunnies, and dirty forgotten socks.

Not to call you a slob but you may grow accustomed to odours which cause others' senses to reel. Everyone can overlook clutter at times, growing used to it until it becomes the norm. Keep in mind that it's not her 'norm'. Change your sheets, pillowcases, and comforter or spread even if you just changed them the night before. If a fragrant spray was purchased, lightly spray sheets first and then pillowcases. Trap the aroma by making your bed before spraying the newly furnished comforter. You do not need much. The carpet can be lightly scented with the same fragrance. A sensual atmosphere is reached when lighting is softened. Try a lightly tinted bulb of low wattage to replace bright lights. You could also remove the ceiling light completely and choose a lamp instead. Why? Because you don't want to have to leave her and cut the lights off. With a lamp, you can reach over and quickly extinguish the soft glow or leave it on for a while. If using candles, make sure they are well away from window treatments and not left alone while lit. When travelling to her place, bring accessories in case you stay overnight. If no previous discussions regarding an all-night stay have taken place, leave the items in your vehicle. Besides the common tools (toothbrush, razor, pyjamas, etc.), some overlooked items are soap (she may use a feminine fragrant blend), condoms or lubricant, and a change of clothing.

Tip: Don't use baby oil as a lubricant. Look for a water-based lubricant or oil intended for sexual activity. Bring a fresh package of condoms along with lubricant. If you're within your bedroom, don't use that three-month-old box in your bedside drawer and the half-full bottle of previously used lubricant.

Even though you both start the evening with clear intentions, you shouldn't move toward the bedroom right away. Let the evening naturally unfold. Nerves or cold feet may set in so further finessing could be required. Of course, if she launches herself at you or shows wantonness (rubbing hips against you, roaming hands, or sends your mind reeling from kisses); begin heading in the bedroom's direction. Since you never know what part of her will greet your eager member, make sure it's especially groomed. You do not want her encountering anything unsavoury (including stubble from a morning groom). Even though all senses of the human bodies are designed to drive arousal higher, you don't know if your particular essence of male will trigger all her senses. Suggestion: dab a small amount of aftershave, cologne, or deodorant on the inside of your thighs in case her nose journeys anywhere within your member's vicinity. Don't use too much because you'll blanket your natural scent which is meant to arouse. Always remain alert to any roommates or people sharing her space. Rules for bathroom, fridge space, or long-term parking may apply. You want no part of an angry roommate pounding on a bedroom door during your moves. Also, don't suddenly exit her bedroom for a drink while in your birthday suit.

Try music

Gentle music can enable you to get within the disposition. But don't forget, the prime focus is on her, not you. Determine the music you love, but additional songs that are sensual, calm, and slow. Consult them in advance concerning their taste in music. Attempt to record on a brand name that you love but select the slower songs of theirs. Quicker pop songs place you inside dance instead of a sensual disposition.

Let's Dance

You have successfully wooed her into climbing nude between your fragrant sheets. Before tearing that condom open with your teeth, start exploring. Her heightened anticipation from your date should move things along quickly. Her pleasure (along with yours) is of the utmost importance to ensure a repeat performance. Unless your closeness allowed for discussion regarding previous partners, you don't know anything regarding her last sexual act. With this in mind, be conscious of any pain or discomfort you may cause.

If she does require a break, be thoughtful and understanding. This does not imply sex is now over (or maybe whatever bad) but that you might be way too much to handle. If something develops together with your member's performance, or maybe you think it is difficult to manage yourself, you might have to go for a pause. Various reasons (age, alcohol, stress, etc.) can adversely affect either of you. Then again, things may progress smoothly and affect you both at the same time. If you reach climax before her, make sure you use previously learned techniques to satisfy her. Afterwards, don't leap out of bed and head out with false emergency issues. If a true emergency does happen, you want to reassure her by calling to let her know whatever the result. You've just experienced your most intimate night. You'll want to keep her informed to set up the next period of play.

Choose the best body words to flirt

Confident and direct body words can mean curiosity. Pick signals to display the female with which you uncover her interest and attractiveness only in a lot more. Remain upright, Keep the head of yours directly as well as your shoulders pulled returned. Don't cross your arms or even keep your drink deep in front of your chest. A signal of almost any type which you're sure of. Locate methods to flirt via the contact screen. Use the female near the hands and also point her throughout the bar or perhaps thru the home in which you met. Or maybe guidebook her by adding your hand on her back. Attempt to steadily obtain the female used to your touch.

Fact Versus Myths

The following section offers some facts in which time and controversy have blurred regarding women's sexuality. Vaginal orgasm is not a myth. With that being said, many women cannot experience the same level of release that clitoral stimulation offers. Besides, most erotica or romantic stories may depict yearning for well-hung members but (in reality) most women become anxious at the sight of such. If you dwell within that category, you'll want to tailor your evening toward relaxation as well as anticipation. Don't fret whatever your size because, by now, you've proven your attentiveness.

Erogenous zones are located under her ears, along her neck, down her back, and a variety of other areas. Dependent upon her level of arousal, her entire skin may become sensitized upon your touch. Unfortunately, some men still believe that a woman's clitoris is located elsewhere. Rest assured, it dwells between her legs and is a target for the climax. Don't get too rough but, at the same time, don't avoid it. Similar to your testicles, this region holds a massive amount of nerves. Lacking G-spots is another myth. Women's vaginas are ridged with these extremely sensitive zones.

After Sex

That's right you aren't done yet. As stated previously, don't rush off. Most women like to cuddle in the afterglow. Give a few minutes and ask her if she wishes to shower with you. If she

314

immediately leaves the bed, ask if you can shower with her. This time will allow you to reinforce the connection and assure yourself as well as her that both have been thoroughly pleased. If you leave afterwards without spending the night, call her when you get home. If she leaves your place, ask that she call you and let you know she arrived safely. This's not really a proposition of any kind, though, a straightforward link exhibiting the gentle side of yours. You might also want to have her on a prolonged journey shortly. You need her to have confidence in you. Allow her to recognize that you've got your best interests under consideration. She requires a guarantee of the place of her inside your potential planet and the bed of yours, including with no has of matrimony.

ABOUT THE AUTHOR

Now, first of all, I am not unlike any other guy out there. I was not born with special talents or gifts— and everything I have right now I had to earn and learn.

In high school, I was a "C" student, not too attractive or interactive, didn't have a lot of friends. And as I'm thinking right now, not really sure why.

Anyway, there was one thing that bothered me a lot, which later on turned into my passion and career choice- since almost every guy in high school had had a relationship, I didn't have one, no matter how bad I wanted. I even tried a few times to go ask for a date or just have a "nice" conversation with a girl. But trust me, you don't want to see how that looked like.

And maybe because of those few failures, I became obsessed about understanding women and having a relationship. So I kept going…

I was reading books, watching videos, and every time I learned something new I went out and tried it out – I didn't know any better. And you know what? Some of them worked! I went to a couple of successful dates, and since then, I was hooked. Not only by women but also by those techniques that were working almost every single time.

Just a few years ago, I decided to share my knowledge with others and pass my skills and knowledge. I began doing one-on-one consultations, and the results my clients got motivated me to go even further and start writing content and reach even more people.

And that's what I just began doing…

I set my goal to help every man who wants to forget about lonely days and experience life full of pleasure and abundance.

I hope that you are going to take a lot from my books and use that knowledge to benefit your life!

HOW TO SEDUCE WOMEN

Printed in Great Britain
by Amazon

44210603R00189